Bloomsday

Bloom

nsday

by
Saul Field
and
Morton Levitt

NEW YORK GRAPHIC SOCIETY • GREENWICH, CONNECTICUT

Standard Book Number 8212-0451-3 (Regular edition)

Standard Book Number 8212-0492-0 (Limited edition)

Library of Congress Catalog Card Number 72-80414

Illustrations © Saul Field 1972

All rights reserved. No part of this book may be reproduced without the written permission of the publisher.

Text quotations from ULYSSES, by James Joyce. Copyright 1914, 1918 by Margaret Caroline Anderson and renewed 1942, 1946 by Nora Joseph Joyce. Reprinted by permission of Random House, Inc.

The Publishers wish to acknowledge the gracious assistance of Mr. Ben Wolf of Leary's Publishing Company, Philadelphia. His discernment and enthusiasm for "Bloomsday" have done much to make this book possible.

A Portrait of James Joyce

For Jean and Annette

This book was designed by Ray Ripper.

The typeface used is 16/17 Trump, set by York Type/Peter Pica, Inc., New York, New York.

The book has been printed in five-color offset lithography and bound by Fabag + Druckerei Winterthur AG, Switzerland.

Printed in Switzerland

Deceived by his wife, reviled by his neighbors, betrayed by his memories, Leopold Bloom is a twentieth-century Ulysses, the representative of a world without heroism. Despite his weaknesses—or perhaps because of them—he emerges from James Joyce's *Ulysses* as the first modern man, a hero for our times. Born a Jew in Catholic Dublin, he is inevitably an alien. He observes his neighbors from outside, is kept by them on the fringes of their society and condemned for his differences. Yet he finds no security even in his Jewishness. A devoted family man, he is knowingly cuckolded by his wife and at one point even seeks a new lover for her; he must send his young daughter from home to protect her from the influence of her mother; he can father no living son to whom to pass on his heritage.

He fails as a businessman, fails as a lover, fails as a surrogate father for the young man he befriends—even his admirable deeds become comic incidents. An advertising rate salesman with ties to a local newspaper, he loses as many commissions as he earns on a representative day; he conducts a futile romance with a mature woman through a pseudonym and a post office box, and the young girl who excites him on the beach turns out to his dismay to be crippled; he visits a neighbor in a lying-in hospital and in an excess of sympathy himself suffers labor pains.

But this is his book, this day—June 16, 1904—his day, known to the world as Bloomsday. He is the hero, not Molly, his wife, whose closing soliloquy is one of the great tours de force of literature; not even Stephen Dedalus, whom we already know from *A Portrait of the Artist as a Young Man*, ostensibly based on Joyce's own life and character. Stephen rejects Bloom in the end but takes away with him a vision of humanity that he has not known before. He is no longer a would-be artist for he now has a subject. And he will write the most influential of modern novels with the most moving hero—Bloom's novel, *Ulysses.*

It is customary for students of Joyce to seek in his works for their bio-

Introduction

graphical sources. Thus, we find signs of the author's own life in the character of Stephen and see his youthful friends and acquaintances in the populace of his fictional city. We use the novel, in short, as a signpost to the historical town. And Joyce is certainly one of the most autobiographical of novelists using somewhere in his fiction nearly everything he knew—and he knew a great deal—as well as virtually everyone he had encountered. There are stories of his friends' fear that they would inadvertently give him something to use in his work. At least one later wrote a book denying that he was the scoundrel whom Joyce had depicted. And we hear of him making notes on whatever happened to be at hand—on the inside of matchbooks, even on his shirt cuffs. But Stephen is not Joyce, and we risk missing the point of the novel—and of *A Portrait* as well—if we confuse them. Many of the details of his life are surely based on that of his creator, but Joyce has not hesitated to change the facts or alter the character to make them fit his conception of the young, developing artist—an outsider devoted entirely to his art, cut off from family, religion and country. He is the young Joyce as Joyce might have been with the perspective of another decade of experience—but he is not Joyce himself. Nor is Bloom Joyce, although Bloom too shows signs of his creator.

It has also become a critical cliché that *Ulysses* could serve as a road map of Dublin at the start of the century, that some future archaeologist could map out almost the entire city, if every other trace of it were to vanish, on the basis of the novel alone. There are Joyceans even today who follow the path of Bloom as he moves through the city, no longer the charming Georgian town it was then but a crowded, bustling, modern capital—still small enough, still enough unchanged that we sense it surely must have been like this for Bloom on a certain spring day in 1904. For we never doubt that he too walked here; we never for a moment question his reality. (A few enthusiasts convert their odyssey into an hegira, following religiously the events of Bloomsday even to burning kidney for breakfast.) It is a delight to wander through Dublin knowing that Bloom too once walked these streets. But we must remember that this physical search is a game, that the reality for us is in the novel *Ulysses.*

Joyce himself left Dublin in 1904 at the age of twenty-two, returning only a few times thereafter and never again after 1912. His entire adult life was thus spent on the Continent in such cities as Rome, Trieste, Paris and Zurich. Yet he consistently returned to Dublin in his fiction; it is the setting for all of his work, made more vital in art than it ever had been in life. Long after number 7 Eccles Street has been torn down Leopold Bloom will continue to climb over its railing on a day when he has left home keyless. There are those who insist that Joyce erred in numbering the row houses of Eccles Street, that Bloom actually lived in number 8. The fiction has become so real for them that they confuse it with that other reality so often lived less vitally. Joyce used Dublin we are told because in his day it was large enough to be cosmopolitan yet small enough for a man to be known by his neighbors so that one of its citizens could become representative of urban man in the West in the twentieth century. Thus, we are not really concerned to know the names of the men upon whom Bloom may have been modeled. He may have some of their parts—as he had some of Joyce's—but for us his reality surpasses theirs. They live at least in part because he has a life of his own.

This perspective of art and life in *Ulysses* may also help us to understand the superstructure of myth on which Joyce has erected his story. As the title suggests, the frame of the novel is the myth of the wanderer Ulysses (or Odysseus, as he is known in Homer's original), the great Greek hero who took ten years to return after the end of the war in Troy to his wife Penelope and his home on the island of Ithaca. The truly small world of Homeric Greece serves as a microcosm of the whole civilized world, and Ulysses is its representative figure—wise and heroic, beloved of the gods, above all, indomitable. In the modern world, Bloom is Ulysses—but ironically. His lesser status is a sign of our own fall from greatness. In the epic of Homer, Penelope resists all of her suitors and faithfully waits for her husband's return; in Joyce's version, Molly Bloom spends the day with her lover and her husband not only knows of it, but suspects that she has had many more. In the original tale, Telemachus searches throughout the mainland for his father and eventually aids him in ridding the house of the suitors; in the modern narrative, Stephen rejects his own drunken father and seeks for a surrogate in Bloom whose own son has died in infancy. The princess Nausicaa becomes the banal and crippled shopgirl Gerty MacDowell; the monstrous Cyclops is now the drunken, anti-Semitic Citizen; the wisdom of Nestor, strategist of the Greek army, turns into the foolishness of the schoolmaster Mr. Deasy.

Joyce named the chapters of the novel for the characters and incidents of the epic; we move from "Telemachus" as Stephen sets out on his search and "Calypso" as we first meet Molly to "The Cave of the Winds" at the newspaper office and "Circe" at Bella Cohen's whorehouse in Nighttown through, finally, to "Ithaca" and "Penelope." But we do not need to recognize all the Homeric parallels to understand *Ulysses*—any more than we need to know the colors or art forms or organs of the body that Joyce supposedly associated with each of the chapters of the novel. The myth does not exist for its own sake so we can test our knowledge against the brilliance of the creator. Its purpose is to lead us to knowledge of the modern predicament and of our own situation in a world suddenly bereft of Homeric glories; to lead us in the end to Bloom—to ourselves.

For Bloom does finally emerge as heroic. We see at last that he is a great man, that he surmounts his weaknesses and rises, albeit unknowingly, above his fellow citizens. He is constantly confusing the scientific data he learned in his public schooling, but we note that he is almost alone in being always curious about the facts of his world. He is impotent with his wife, stays away from home to avoid her lover and returns to a typically crumby welcome (for Boylan, her lover, has been eating in bed and Joyceans, like Joyce, can never resist a pun); yet Molly respects him as husband and father. He mourns the suicide of his father Rudolph and the death of his infant son Rudy for without them his life has lost much of its value; but he continues to live with interest and vigor and to look for meaning in life. He is the victim of a vicious anti-Semitic attack although he is uncertain about his own religious identification for he has somehow been baptized both as a Protestant and as a Catholic. Each of the many Jewish references he makes on this day is marked by some error, yet we come to recognize his unique sense of identity, a sense that he himself does not quite understand. To his neighbors he is a figure of scorn or of comedy, but we realize what they do not, that here is a man of true compassion, that Bloom has an unconscious dignity that rivals Ulysses'. His greatness is hardly heroic, but it may be all that we today can attain to.

This is the Bloom that Saul Field gives us in his *Bloomsday Suite,* a conception very nearly as rich and varied and original as that of Joyce himself. It was almost inevitable that Field would discover Bloom, for he had earlier been drawn to the stories of Sholem Aleichem and especially to the character of Tevye the milkman, another "schlemiel" hero, another victim who somehow retains his dignity in a world without dignity. Field is an artist, not a literary expert, and he recognizes in Bloom that quality of character and experience that is common to all men—our fear of absurdity and failure, our striving for dignity and meaning in life, our common humanity.

Joyce himself was far more interested in music than he was in the visual arts. That is why he made Molly a concert singer and why snatches of song, both popular and serious, run perpetually through the minds of Leopold and Stephen. (Nora Joyce always suspected that her husband had chosen the wrong career, that he should have been a singer and not a writer.) Saul Field thus brings to *Ulysses* an original visual perspective that not even Joyce could have predicted. All great works of literature are capable of new interpretation—that is one major proof of their greatness. The scholars and critics have had their say about *Ulysses;* it is time now for other artists to interpret the novel, to do for *Ulysses* what Joyce has done for the *Odyssey* of Homer. And this Field does brilliantly. The *Bloomsday Suite* makes accessible in a new form— and to some for the first time—a work that many abandon for fear of new failure. We have given over this greatest of novels to the scholars and critics because we suspected its difficulty, but Field makes it available, reveals a Bloom whom we all need to know, whom we should have known all along.

#7 Eccles St.

Home for Bloom is number 7 Eccles St., "Sr. ecles" in the Gaelic. It is here that his day begins with joyful relish and here that it ends in the sadness of nighttime and old memories. Every step on his odyssey in between is directed to his return to this solid, conventional, lower-middle-class residence. It serves as implicit symbol throughout the novel, the central visible sign of stability in Bloom's life, and is as dear to him as longed-for Ithaca is to the adventurer Odysseus. It even exerts a certain influence on Molly whose infamous exploits take place entirely within its walls, suggesting that they may be less spectacular in deed than they are reputed to be in legend. From its bedroom windows, Molly peers out at the world around her, her view of humanity totally different from that of her husband yet strangely overlapping it.

Bloom's day begins with a trip to Dlugacz the pork butcher where he buys the kidney that he will inadvertently burn for breakfast and where he picks up the handbill whose imagery will pursue him throughout the day: it advertises Agendath Netaim, "the model-farm at Kinnereth on the lakeshore of Tiberias," a Zionist reclamation settlement in Palestine someday to be planted with orange groves and melon fields, trees of eucalyptus and almonds, olives and citron. But a cloud covers the sun as Bloom reads and he envisions instead the Holy Land as it is now:

> *A barren land, bare waste,...the dead sea....A dead sea in a dead land, grey and old. Old now. It bore the oldest, the first race....The oldest people. Wandered far away over all the earth, captivity to captivity, multiplying, dying, being born everywhere. It lay there now. Now it could bear no more.*

He attributes this dread vision to "Morning mouth bad images. Got up wrong side of the bed," and he wonders if resuming his morning exercises will exorcise them. But its cause, we come to recognize, is more immediate, more closely tied to the heart of Bloom's predicament—to

No. 7 Eccles Street

his son Rudy, dead long ago in infancy, to his confused sense of his own Jewishness, to his identity as eternal wanderer and alien in this place where he was born. All this becomes apparent, however, only as the day wears on and Bloom's psychological defenses fade along with the light—only when he returns home again to Ithaca.

Recreated here is number 9 Eccles St., for number 7 has long since fallen victim to the decay which besets most of Georgian Dublin. Field endeavors in this engraving to recapture that former beauty as it must have been, as it appears to us in *Ulysses*. And so he creates the graceful window shades and water pipe and the jewel-like railings that Bloom later will climb on his return to Eccles St., for he has left home keyless on this fine June day—an apparent sign of his rootlessness, but one that we already suspect may be misleading. And it is his ghostlike memory of his wife—whose image was inspired by an actress Field once saw in a stage production of "Ulysses in Nighttown"—which dominates Bloom's home as it dominates his consciousness throughout the day. That is why the image extends beyond the edge of the plate and why there are so many loose strands of fabric around her—to suggest the stream of Bloom's consciousness. This same vision of Molly appears elsewhere in the *Bloomsday Suite* but in different versions: the same image, but used in new ways and with new contexts. Field calls them second and third generation plates. But for Bloom, without father or son, there will be no new generation, no Rudy to be for Leopold "what Leopold was for Rudolph." Not family continuity but the physical presence of his home seems to represent stability to Bloom.

Leopold Bloom and the Nymph

On the wall above the Blooms' wedding bed is a picture entitled "The Bath of the Nymph," distributed free with the Easter issue of *Photo Bits* magazine. (The frame, however, cost three and six.) To Leopold's admiring eye, the nymph recalls a slimmer Molly with her hair down as she was in the first days of their marriage, and he uses her to explain the meaning of "metempsychosis" to his wife. Molly has come across the term while reading in bed, pronouncing it "met-him-pike-hoses," and Bloom with characteristic patience at her ignorance and a certain intellectual curiosity of his own attempts to answer her question. In the process, he reveals something of his own nature.

"It's Greek," he says, frowning, "from the Greek. That means the transmigration of souls." "O, rocks!" she responds. "Tell us in plain words." So Bloom thinks of the naked nymphs of ancient Greece and of the people who lived at that time, and then instead of speaking of human souls, distracted perhaps by the picture before him, he explains that a nymph is a woman who has been changed into an animal or tree. He is interrupted at this point by the smell of burnt kidney from the kitchen, the lure of the flesh in a sense drawing him still further from discussion of the soul. His explanation, moreover, is only partially correct. Nymphs are indeed personifications of natural forces and in some myths they are metamorphosed into animals or trees, or even into rivers or mountains. But the change that Bloom envisions has nothing to do with metempsychosis; his is a transformation of bodies and not one of souls. The nymph over the bed, probably a naiad, may well represent the river or lake in which she is bathing, but she can hardly be seen as a symbol of the immortal soul of mankind. This is not the only time that Bloom will mistake body for soul; his minor errors of fact turn frequently into such potential distortions.

Virtually every intellectual exercise that Bloom sets for himself is similarly resolved—with curiosity, with partial understanding, with some final confusion or incompletion. As a scientist, for example, he wonders

Leopold Bloom and the Nymph

on his walk to the butcher in the morning sun while wearing a black suit whether "Black conducts, reflects (refracts is it?) the heat"; as a man of letters, he attributes the "Eulogy in a country churchyard" to Thomas Campbell or Wordsworth; as a man of affairs, he is naive about Irish politics and full of impractical economic schemes; as a communicant of various religions, he displays little knowledge of Catholicism, no interest at all in Protestantism and a great deal of confusion about Judaism. Part of his problem is a defective memory, as he acknowledges himself. Typically, he refers to it as his "mnemotechnic"; "he never can explain a thing the way a body can understand," Molly complains. He manages somehow to exaggerate the significance of every mental chore that confronts him.

We are inclined as a result to laugh at Bloom's shallow pretensions and perhaps even to scorn him until we realize that aside from the equally isolated Stephen Dedalus he is the only resident of this fictional city to demonstrate any real curiosity about the world around him, to be concerned about its functions and meaning. The intellectuals who gather in the National Library, the gentlemen of the press and those who inhabit the public houses of Dublin, the people of the streets—even Stephen to a certain extent—are locked into a world of set ideas and narrow conventions. Bloom alone rises above their parochialism; he alone among them is willing to listen to new ideas and anxious to learn. His openness and curiosity lead us almost begrudgingly, and surely with surprise, to treat his intellect with a certain respect. His is hardly the cunning of "quick-witted" Odysseus that "man of many ruses" so beloved of grey-eyed Athene, but in our diminished times it will have to do.

In the Homeric analogue, the nymph suggests Calypso the divine seducer who kept far-travelled Odysseus at her bedside for seven long years. In this engraving she is also one of the many guises of Molly, presented both realistically and in a stylized fashion. Field's technique is again akin to Joyce's own narrative method. For Ulysses functions on at least two distinct levels of meaning: the realistic on the one hand on which we read of the surface events of urban life in the West at the start of the century, a tale of missed connections among masses of people; and on the other hand a symbolic level on which we see the psychological forces at work beneath this widespread communications failure and discover certain positive forces persisting alongside them. A first reading of the novel is almost invariably limited to the surface, realistic level. That is what one critic meant when he commented that we cannot read *Ulysses* for the first time—we can only reread it. And Molly appears throughout the narrative in two almost distinct guises, as we see her directly through her own point of view and as her husband perceives her. We get a sense of both in this engraving.

The novel is also filled with private jokes. It is no accident that the nymph, subject of a misguided discussion about spiritual rebirth, was distributed with the Easter issue of a cheap magazine. In the engraving, the lettering for the erotic text was done by Saul Field's daughter, Martina, who was five years old at the time.

Blazes Boylan and Molly

In Bloom's somewhat clouded eyes, Blazes Boylan is not the first of Molly's lovers but only one "in a series originating in and repeated to infinity." There are twenty-four alleged predecessors to Boylan on his mental list, including two priests, the Lord Mayor of Dublin and a bootblack in the General Post Office. Some of these "lovers" are so improbable, however, and Bloom offers so little proof of their complicity that we may suspect that Boylan after all is the first. Of him there can be no doubt.

Boylan is the promoter who is arranging Molly's next concert tour, and he is coming that afternoon with the program. Bloom himself brings up the letter announcing the visit to Molly in bed and he watches her tuck it warily beneath her pillow. He reacts with strange equanimity. Certainly he is jealous, even envious of the "bold hand" which addresses his wife. But no man is more reasonable than Bloom, no man can more evenly evaluate the situation. After all, he reasons, he cannot assassinate Boylan; he is no man—and this is no time—for duel by combat; and it is too late in the game for divorce. Moreover, he understands his wife's weakness, for it is eleven years since he has slept with her—since the death in infancy of Rudy, their son.

Bloom stays away from home during the day in order to avoid his wife's lover. Yet in a city like Dublin, he is bound to run constantly into reminders of his presence. There are Boylan's friends and those who ask, perhaps innocently, about the concert tour; there are the advertising men who work for him and spread his name; and there is Boylan himself as viewed from a funeral carriage, on the steps of the library—Bloom ducks into the Museum to avoid him and here crosses Stephen's path—in the bar of the Ormond Hotel; even his daughter Milly mentions him in her letter from Mullingar, unaware that her father has sent her to work away from home to keep her innocent of Boylan. And as Bloom walks through the streets of the city, he hears in his imagination the incessant jingle jangle of his wedding bed on Eccles Street.

Blazes Boylan and Molly

Boylan, he thinks, is the "worst man in Dublin," the antithesis of all that he himself represents, and he wonders about the fascination that he holds for Molly. But she knows Boylan for the most eligible bachelor in the city and she is proud that he has chosen her and not some delicate lady. Nor is she alone in her admiration: the barmaids at the Ormond Hotel also play up to him and the girl who waits on him in a flower shop blushes under his gaze. It is here that he plucks the red carnation that he later grasps between his smiling teeth.

It is this "jingle jaunty blazes boy" who is captured in this engraving. Debonair, self-assured, confident of his charm, he is the very model of a certain type of Irishman. And so he is clothed not in the black serge suit described in the novel, but entirely in green—even to his complexion. And the flower between his sardonic teeth is not the carnation from Thornton's flower shop but a rose, suggesting the rose of Castile that both Molly and Bloom recall from their courtship—Molly with a rose in her hair lying for the first time with Bloom among the rhododendrons on the Hill of Howth outside Dublin.

Behind Boylan is a web of cloth, suggesting the widespread web of his influence and providing a shadowy background to his most forceful personality. The uncontrolled loose strands of the fabric may also symbolize the unconscious mind, not of Boylan but of Bloom, who is so obsessed with his rival.

Molly's relationship with her lover is suggested by the perspective of the figures in the print. Molly with her vulpine face lies quiet, accepting and small at Boylan's feet. The contrast with "Leopold Bloom and the Nymph" is striking: there it is Bloom who is subdued and tiny, while the goddess—another figure of Molly—is aggressive and huge.

In Molly's magnificent soliloquy which closes the novel, it is Boylan and his flower which first occupy her but the rose of Bloom which she recalls at the end. For even she recognizes in the end his greater substance. Boylan may have wonderful form, but it is the depth and humanity of Bloom that we remember. And the image of Boylan that remains is as Bloom sees him passing on to his assignation:

> *By Bachelor's walk jogjaunty jingled Blazes Boylan, bachelor, in sun, in heat, mare's glossy rump atrot, with flick of whip, on bounding tyres: sprawled, warmseated, Boylan impatience, ardentbold.*

The foremost comic image in the *Bloomsday Suite* is this act of the imagination, Bloom wearing the horns of a cuckold and waving aloft the flag of his wife's infidelity. It is the only image of Bloom that some of his neighbors are able to recognize and in this sense may tell us as much about them as it does about him. The artistic method, moreover, offers a surprisingly apt insight into Joyce's technique and the literary revolution that he began.

We, of course, are aware of Boylan almost from the start, and there are hints throughout the day that others may also know of his relations with Molly. Surely everyone knows his reputation and in a perverse way even takes pride in him, like some member of the club, as if his sensuality somehow amplified each man's capacity. They are equally willing to think the worst of the outsider Bloom. (The sole exception to this is Martin Cunningham, and he, we may remember from *Dubliners,* has marital problems of his own.) Bloom, in any event, is fearful of what these people may believe of Molly and him. Yet he cannot be sure what they believe—as when he meets M'Coy, whose wife is also a singer, and speaks with him of concert tours and the death that week of poor Paddy Dignam. When M'Coy asks suddenly of Mrs. Bloom's health his question seems innocent enough to us, but Bloom notices a change in his tone. Is it a change from speaking of death to social amenities, or is it a change from respect to innuendo? We may suspect that Bloom is overly sensitive but he simply cannot be certain, and since we are limited to his point of view—since we can know no more than he of his friend's implication—we too must admit the dual possibilities. Such is the ambiguity that marks the whole world of *Ulysses,* a sense of uncertainty about all the aspects of life, representing a violent break both with the narrative techniques of the Victorians and with their vision of life.

The Victorians were the last generation to seem totally confident of their ability to comprehend and resolve every problem confronting them, and the fiction of the time reflected this certainty. Victorian

The Antlered Hatrack

novelists were expected to demonstrate absolute mastery over the lives of their characters, to know events even beyond the confines of their novels and to take their readers into their confidence at all significant times. Thus we have Thackeray referring to himself as the "Manager of the Performance" and to the characters of *Vanity Fair* as his "Puppets." Thus too the final chapters of virtually all of Dickens' novels take place two, or five or even ten years after the action has ended and inform the readers of what has happened in the interim to those characters whom they had come to know and to love. There was even talk of an act in Parliament to ask Mr. Dickens not to kill off Little Nell, the wretched young heroine of *The Old Curiosity Shop.* This intimate relationship among novelist, characters and audience reflected a view of a totally coherent universe, one that never truly existed in fact. For close beneath this seemingly amiable surface were the evils of the Industrial Revolution; typically, the Victorians presumed that even these evils could be resolved. By the summer of 1915, with the realization that a new kind of warfare had destroyed forever the old hopes and values, this final illusion was also shattered. Since that time, the insights of such eminent Victorians as Darwin, Marx, Einstein and Freud have helped to remake our world and have convinced us unalterably that such a worldview will never again be supportable. Victorian confidence—along with the omniscience of Victorian authors—has been replaced for us by a new ambiguity.

Joyce was one of the first to perceive this truth, even before the outbreak of the war. There is a line in *A Portrait of the Artist as a Young Man*, first published in 1914, which might almost serve as epigraph to the new sensibility: "The artist," Stephen Dedalus proclaimed, "like the God of the creation, remains within or behind or beyond or above his handiwork, invisible, refined out of existence, indifferent, paring his fingernails." In this new novel that Stephen would write, there would be no special relationship between author and reader, no omniscient voice

The Antlered Hatrack in the Hall

informing us what to believe, no sense that the universe is made easily coherent. We can measure the effect of this change, its influence on contemporary fiction and on our view of the world, by examining one representative novel, a work that would not have been possible without this insight of Stephen and Joyce.

In Alain Robbe-Grillet's *The Voyeur* (English version published in 1958), we are faced with a man who rapes and kills a thirteen-year-old girl or who watches as someone else kills her or who thinks he has seen someone commit the crime, or who suspects he may have done so himself. There is even a chance that the entire event is set sometime in the future, that the ferryboat on which the protagonist is riding at the end of the novel is taking him to the scene of the crime and not away from it. And while the young girl does have a name, she is but one of more than a dozen possible victims including a girl glimpsed in a window on the way to the ferry, another pictured in a newspaper clipping and a dressmaker's dummy. The protagonist is himself so confused, his view of the world around him so distorted by possibilities, that he cannot interpret. We too—because we are again limited exclusively to his point of view—may be uncertain not only of the meaning behind the events but of the action itself. We know for sure only that he is a psychopath who might have committed the crime and that such deeds are somehow consistent with our new civilization.

Such is the revolution foreshadowed by a chance encounter in a Dublin street. The world of *The Voyeur* is hardly one that Bloom would appreciate yet this one too he could learn to live with. For himself, he would surely prefer the simpler vision of Victorian certainty, but he knows too well that there really are no easy solutions, that ambiguity is always the order of the day. For now, however, he continues to walk the streets of his city, fearful that others will perceive the burden he bears on his figurative horns, knowing all the time that the real panties are in his pocket.

Paddy Dignam's Funeral

At eleven o'clock in the morning of June 16, Martin Cunningham, Jack Power, Simon Dedalus and Leopold Bloom enter the carriage that will take them to Glasnevin cemetery for the funeral of their friend Paddy Dignam. As they ride through the outskirts of the city continuing Bloom's odyssey, they pass familiar sights and well-known figures, among them Stephen Dedalus on his way to Sandymount beach. This is just the first of many times that his path and Bloom's will cross, and each time the bonds between them will grow: Stephen-Telemachus in search of a spiritual father and Odysseus-Bloom, lacking a son to succeed him. Even Molly by the end of the day will think of Stephen as a possible surrogate for her own dead son.

His companions begin speaking of death, but Bloom in his thoughts rejects their sentimentality. He too mourns Dignam, but he knows that his friend died of too much cheap whiskey and not simply of a sudden heart attack; he will not speak of Rudy to them, but we recognize that he must scorn Simon Dedalus' sanctimonious claim that a dead child is "well out of" this life; and as they talk of suicide, he sits in silence, unthinking, watching the kindly face of Martin Cunningham (who argues that men cannot judge the heart of the suicide), rejecting the Christian cruelty toward those who take their own lives. Cunningham later whispers to Power that Bloom's own father, proprietor of the Queen's Hotel in the town of Ennis, had poisoned himself. Bloom thinks only of that hotel bedroom on the day of the inquest and of the letter "To my dear son Leopold." That letter is still in his drawer, and he will read it that night when he is finally alone among the images of his past. Perhaps he reads it each night of his life.

This is the so-called "Hades" chapter of *Ulysses,* named for the journey that Odysseus takes to the underworld in order to learn of his future and to tie together the strands of his past. For Bloom it creates the first union of Rudolph and Rudy, his dead father and son, and of Leopold with Stephen, who will give immortality to Bloom in a way that he could

I

never anticipate.

In the engraving, all this occurs within the heart, as the hearse approaches the gates of Glasnevin. In the background, in a marvelous compression of space and of time, we see the monument to Roger Casement, the Irish patriot hanged as a traitor by the British in 1916. The figures seated within the heart offer a unique opportunity to view the methods of the artist and his adaptation of the novelist's tools.

This is obviously not a literal effort to reproduce the scene in the carriage, but these shadowy figures do somehow suggest Bloom's companions and perhaps even Leopold himself. All three men are derived from a sketch of Field's friend Harry Pollock, who played Bloom in the Toronto production of "Ulysses in Nighttown." The pen and ink drawing reproduced on the opposite page is that original, the figure on the right taken from life during the performance. The technique which transforms that figure in the engraving is one of those fortuitous accidents that sometimes become the stuff of art.

The technique developed by Field and his wife, the artist Jean Townsend, often employs pieces of cloth onto which a plastic-like compound of the Fields' invention called compotina is poured. When the fabric is of open weave, as when tarleton (a heavy muslin used for cleaning plates) is used, a plain piece of paper is placed beneath it to soak up the excess. Lifting the hardened plate that he had made for this print, Field noticed that the paper beneath it had become what is called a second generation plate, a kind of negative in which lines appeared where there had been open spaces in the positive tarleton image. Field chose this "accident" as his finished plate, recognizing that its unusual texture somehow captured the elusive, almost uncanny atmosphere—we might almost call it texture too—of Joyce's "Hades." And just as this chapter serves in the novel to foreshadow the episodes in that part of Dublin called Nighttown, so this plate prepares us for the hallucinatory effect of "The Ten Shilling House" (page 69). The setting for that print is Bloom's bowler hat, turned upside down, as the artist continued to experiment with different forms of Bloom in action; another sketch in this same series served as the model for "Bella-Bello" (page 77).

"The artist who doesn't understand the importance of accident is not a real artist," the painter David Alfaro Siqueiros once told Saul Field. "He lacks the artistic sensibility." In utilizing this accident with his plate, the printmaker was closer than he realized at the time to the narrative method of Joyce, who well understood the use of the fortuitous event in the midst of an otherwise carefully planned work of art. In his definitive biography, *James Joyce,* Richard Ellmann tells the story of Joyce dictating portions of *Finnegans Wake* to his young friend Samuel Beckett: "In the middle of one such session there was a knock at the door which Beckett didn't hear. Joyce said, 'Come in,' and Beckett wrote it down. Afterwards he read back what he had written and Joyce said, 'What's that "Come in?"' 'Yes, you said that,' said Beckett. Joyce thought for a moment, then said. 'Let it stand.' He was quite willing to accept coincidence as a collaborator." One senses similar possibilities elsewhere in *Finnegans Wake* and in some of the early works of Beckett as well.

Joyce uses his tools—words, sentences, paragraphs, fragments—like an artist working in mosaic. The technique is startlingly like Field's, as Field once described what he called his "jigsaw puzzle effect"..."cutting out my individual images from the background, inking all the plates separately including the background, then inserting the cuts back into their original places before pulling the proof. I could write a book on the multi-variations this process developed.... After getting hooked on Joyce some years later, I learned that he had dubbed this device 'mosaic,' and so I adopted the name for my own. But the guy is slippery as old hell. Since then I've run across another of his names for the device, 'Mah-

Jongg Puzzles!!!'" In both Joyce and Field, the straining for detail—even when it occurs by accident—is really an effort to achieve universality. "In the particular," Joyce once told a young writer, "is contained the universal," and no character in art as both Joyce and Field see him is more particular and universal than Bloom.

There is one possible literary problem in Field's interpretation of "Hades," an instance of taking the novelist too much at his word. Joyce claimed and most critics have agreed that each chapter of *Ulysses* is distinguished by some organ of the body as well as by a characteristic color and prose style. The varying styles are undeniable, but neither the colors nor the organs really perform any significant literary function. Joyce may simply have been trying to forestall the inevitable complaint that his difficult novel was an unstructured fraud; if anything, he told Samuel Beckett, he feared that his work was "oversystematized."

The organ assigned to "Hades" is clearly the heart and Field, for the sole time in the entire *Bloomsday Suite,* chose to utilize Joyce's image rather than to develop his own. A strange phenomenon occurs in the process: what is virtually functionless in prose—the organ of this chapter might as well be Bloom's big left toe or the phallic monument of Casement—becomes significant visually. For this is all interior action, and it does take place ultimately within the heart and not in the mind or senses of Bloom. The artist intuits the image that works for him even when the author—and especially his critics—may have been wrong. We learn increasingly that *Ulysses* can be read with creativity and insight by nearly any reader willing to give himself freely to the task.

Paddy Dignam's Funeral

Paddy Dignam's Funeral — A.P. — Saul Field

In his mind's eye, peering like a voyeur through a keyhole, Bloom visualizes the lovers, romanticizes them, sees them somehow as young and slim and beautiful. This is hardly the Blazes and Molly that we know, however, and nothing at all like her memory of the events of the day:

> ...I was coming for about 5 minutes with my legs around him I had to hug him after O Lord I wanted to shout out all sorts of things fuck or shit or anything at all...O Lord I can't wait till Monday...

Yet even she has some delicacy:

> ...one thing I didn't like his slapping me behind going away so familiarly in the hall though I laughed Im not a horse or an ass am I...

Still, she is no romantic and scorns those "silly women [who] believe love is sighing" as Bloom evidently does.
Bloom has a far different sentiment for Rudy, however, for his dead son represents all those things that his life might have been, the values that he continues to hold despite the hostility that surrounds him and seems to follow him everywhere. His sex life with Molly has ceased with the death of their sole male child, but the memory of Rudy—again romanticized, idealized—remains a sustaining force in Bloom's daily

The Keyhole and Rudy

life. He listens to the parental boasts of "Noisy selfwilled" Simon Dedalus, a poor father yet "Full of his son," and he thinks: "He is right. Something to hand on. If little Rudy had lived. See him grow up. Hear his voice in the house.... My son. Me in his eyes. Strange feeling it would be. From me."

But there will be no son for Leopold Bloom, no one to whom he can pass on whatever heritage he himself has received. And so, as he awaits the birth of a neighbor's child at the Holles St. lying-in hospital, the sterile imagery of Palestine, the home of his ancestors, becomes one in his mind with his vision of Rudy: "Agendath is a waste land, a home of screechowls and the sandblind upupa. Netaim, the golden, is no more." Thus he mourns, in an unconscious paraphrase of Rabbi Hillel, "No son of thy loins is by thee. There is none now to be for Leopold, what Leopold was for Rudolph."

The two images here are really one print, for these are the images that most obsess Bloom, and they seem nearly indistinguishable at times. If they appear romanticized, it is because he has made them so, for both are perceived from his point of view in a kind of visual stream of consciousness: implicit at the keyhole is his figurative eye, and inside his mind we can see quite literally the ideas that dominate his consciousness, the memory of his dead son more important even than his imagined perception of his deceitful wife and her lover.

Blazes and Molly (The Keyhole)

Rudy

Lestrygonians

"Mr. Leopold Bloom ate with relish the inner organs of beasts and fowls." Thus begins the first description of Bloom in *Ulysses,* one which distinguishes him immediately from the intellectual Stephen and sensual Molly. Images of food and places of eating are continually associated with Bloom—from the burnt kidney in the kitchen to the crumbs in his bed—and several episodes in the novel revolve around his gustatory habits. Together, they help to suggest his earthiness, his closeness to the basic functions of life. But even here we learn something of his intellect and spirit.

The scene of "Lestrygonians" (named for the cannibal giants who assault Odysseus' crew) is lunchtime at Burton's restaurant, where men feed like animals at the bar, "swilling, wolfing gobfuls of sloppy food," where the smells too are repellent—"Spaton sawdust, sweetish warmish cigarette smoke, reek of plug, split beer, men's beery piss, the stale of ferment." Bloom looks in at the door but his tastes are too fastidious for this and he goes instead to Davy Byrne's, a "Moral pub," for a light snack of gorgonzola with mustard, some Italian olives and a good glass of burgundy. He eats with moderation and a certain respect for his food, but only a Bloom would use mustard on so distinctive a cheese as gorgonzola.

Later he will dine at the Ormond Hotel and overhear from the bar the bonhomie of Simon Dedalus and his friends—among them Blazes Boylan about to depart for his tryst. Bloom sits quietly as he eats, ruminating over the events of the day, unaware that for him the most important events are still to come, listening to the sounds from the bar. The evocation of Dublin idiom and Dublin song makes the dinner scene (in the "Sirens" chapter) the most lyrical in the entire novel, a lyricism not of subject matter but of sound. Even the structure of "Sirens" is musical, introducing at the start a catalogue of aural motifs. There are fifty-nine of them in all, terms of narrative description, snatches of conversation and song, sounds of the movement of coins and clocks and garters smacking on heavy thighs. Each one is developed in turn until the final crescendo of Bloom's flatulence, caused, he suspects, by the burgundy:

Cyclops

> *Fff. Oo. Rrpr.*
> *...*
> *Pprrpffrrppfff*
> *Done.*

"Among novelists," the music critic Harold Schonberg once wrote, "Joyce knew his music best." And if music provides both sound and structure for Joyce's "Sirens," it is prominent as well in this visualization. The Irish harp in the background of Saul Field's print links "Lestrygonians" with "Sirens" in a way that is itself almost musical, for it serves as symbol of both motifs, of both the food and the music, and of the way of life that they stand for. ("Harp" is also the name of one of the most popular brands of ale in Ireland.)

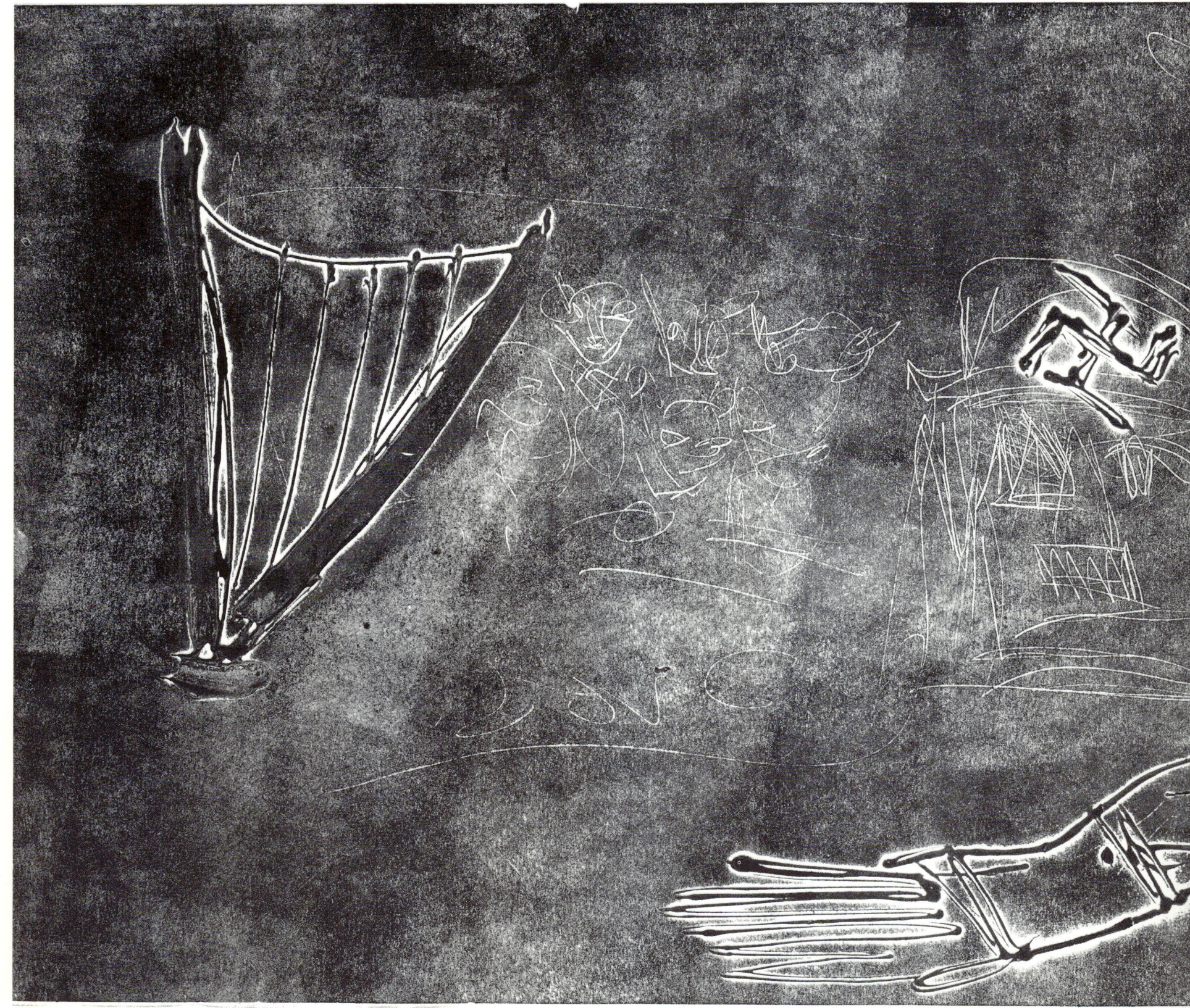

The metamorphosis of men into swine continues in Barney Kiernan's saloon, where Bloom goes to meet Martin Cunningham to arrange for the prompt payment of Dignam's insurance to his widow and children. He meets instead the unnamed patriot known as the Citizen, shot put champion of all Ireland, confirmed chauvinist and hater of all things foreign or Jewish. The Citizen scorns Bloom's reasonableness, his claim to be an Irishman, his obvious differences. In mock-heroic action, he chases the intruder from the saloon, hurling a great object after him. It was a huge rock that the original Cyclops threw at Odysseus' ship; this giant, half-blinded by the sun and his own ignorance, can manage only a biscuit box. The Cyclops stands in the plate below made especially for Field's film of the *Bloomsday Suite* and never pulled as an edition of prints.

The best that Bloom can do in rejoinder to the Citizen's assault is a kind of afterthought, a list of famous men who were Jews: Mendelssohn he names, and Mercadante, Marx and Spinoza, and, oh yes, Jesus—"Your

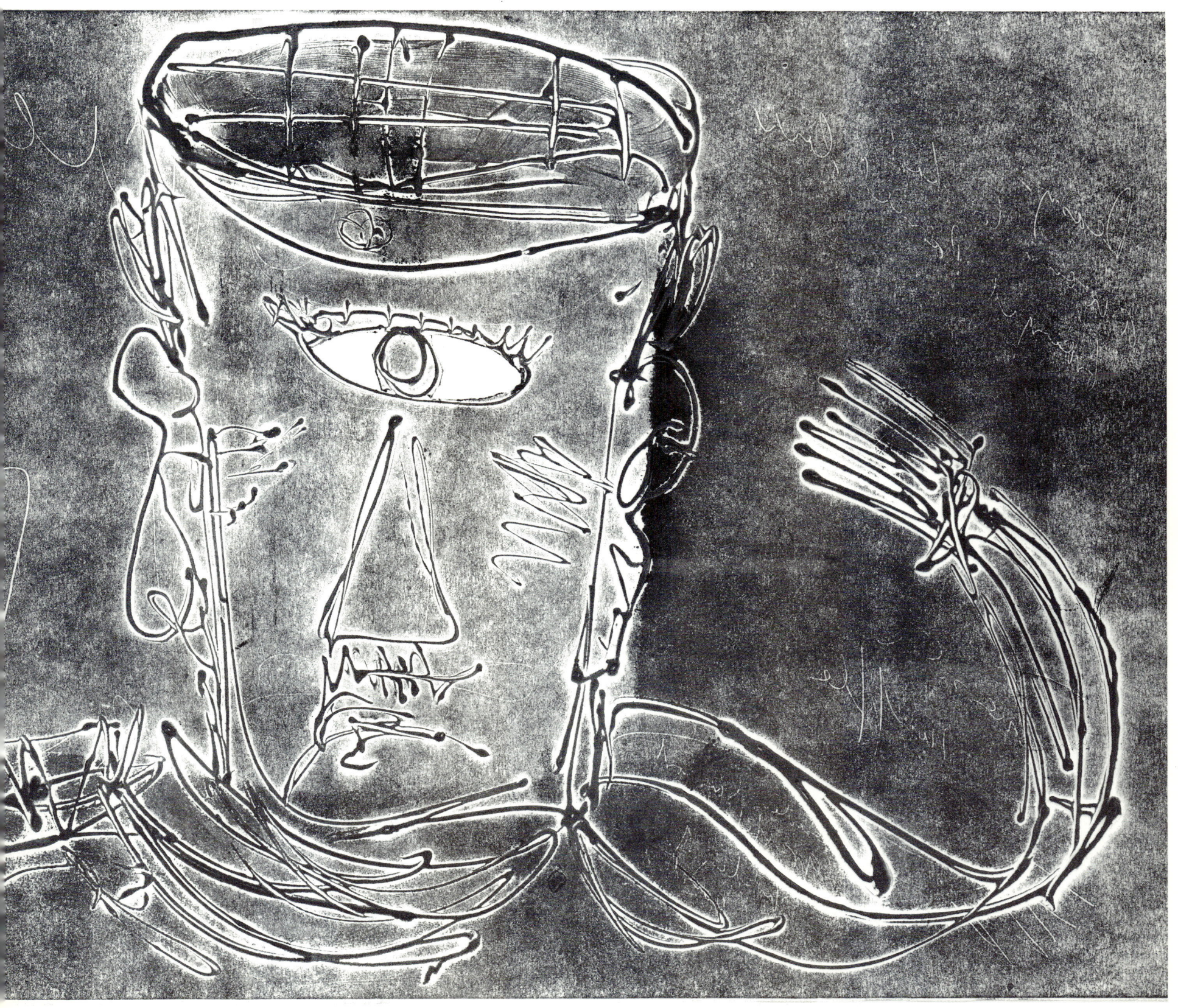

Lestrygonians

God was a jew. Christ was a jew like me," he calls out: Jews converted to Christianity, Jews become anti-Semites, Jews excommunicated by their own congregations; of all those that he names, Christ alone was born and died a Jew. The irony of *Ulysses* cuts in many directions.

In all these scenes, Joyce captures brilliantly the peculiar rhythms of colloquial speech and popular song that we can hear even today in the public houses of Dublin. But Joyce reveals something more as well—a closedmindedness that stifles communication among men, a pretentious heroism that mocks only itself. In the pubs could be found all that Joyce most despised in his homeland—that what might have become great creativity elsewhere was here dissipated in ignorance and drunken camaraderie. Yet, at the same time, he found great charm here. We need only listen with Bloom to the sounds from the bar to recognize that. The tension which arises from this love-hate relationship accounts for much of the power of Joyce's vision of Dublin and its citizenry.

All of this comes together in the harp: traditional symbol of Ireland, it stands in world mythology as a bridge between heaven and earth. "Only the harp," Bloom thinks, listening fatalistically to the sounds of music, seeing Boylan in transit remembering his own courtship of Molly. "We are their harps. I. He. Old. Young." The gods may indeed play with us, as Bloom suggests, and there may well be no heaven connected to earth, yet we alone are responsible for what we become. And it is better to look in at the door with Bloom than to become one of the swine.

Nausicaa

Most of the events of *Ulysses* are perceived, naturally enough, from the points of view of Stephen or Molly or Bloom, but several episodes are presented instead as minor personages view them. In some of these instances, we see the action through several characters at once, one might almost say from the point of view of the community at large. This is especially true of "Wandering Rocks," the chapter depicting three o'clock in the center of town as it is experienced by Father Conmee and Corny Kelleher the undertaker's assistant, by Martin Cunningham and John Wyse Nolan, by the two young daughters of Simon Dedalus and by Boylan's secretary, Miss Dunne. At other times, a single character who may appear nowhere else will present all or most of a chapter. This is the case in "Cyclops," which is narrated by an anonymous barstander, a man full of wit, an acute sense of history and language and just a bit of intolerance himself. It is also true in the "Oxen of the Sun," the hospital sequence in which Joyce parodies the growth and development of the English language and inadvertently makes us aware of his own presence in the narrative. It is also found as well in the first part of "Nausicaa," the events of eight p.m. on Sandymount strand as they are seen by Gerty MacDowell.

In Homer, it is the princess Nausicaa—"so fine in mould and feature that she seemed a goddess"—who shelters the shipwrecked Odysseus and makes it possible for him to return home at last to Ithaca. In some early versions of the myth, the wanderer, strongly attracted himself to Nausicaa, brings her to Ithaca to marry his son and continue the royal line of his land. The Victorian novelist Samuel Butler believed that Nausicaa was in fact the poet who had written the *Odyssey* (there was widespread belief in the nineteenth century that the two epic poems attributed to Homer had actually been composed by two different authors living in far different periods), and Robert Graves' more recent novel, the appropriately titled *Homer's Daughter,* is also based on that theme.

Joyce deals with the tradition, but again, he does so ironically: his

Nausicaa is a crippled shopgirl who finds her wanderer exposed on the beach, excites him sexually from afar and then limps away. Fragile, sentimental, pathetic, Gerty MacDowell is the surest sign of epic decay in our time. She has evidently read all the romantic young ladies' magazines of the day, and they have helped to form her sensibility and intellect; it is their linguistic style and attitude toward life that are reflected in her vision of herself and of Bloom.

We first see Gerty as she visualizes herself, stretched out on the beach, her dress hiked high on her legs: "Her figure was slight and graceful, inclining even to fragility.... The waxen pallor of her face was almost spiritual in its ivorylike purity though her rosebud mouth was a genuine Cupid's bow, Greekly perfect. Her hands were of finely veined alabaster with tapering fingers.... From everything in the least indelicate her finebred nature instinctively recoiled." And we see as well her gentleman onlooker as she romanticizes him: "The eyes that were fastened upon her set her pulses tingling.... Whitehot passion was in that face, passion silent as the grave and it made her his.... [S]he knew he could be trusted to the death, steadfast, a sterling man, a man of inflexible honour to his fingertips."

But Leopold Bloom romanticizes in a far different way: excited as her dress hikes higher and higher, his passions rising along with his eyes as Roman candles climax in the sky above them, he masturbates with his hand in his pocket. Impotent with his wife, like Onan he spills his seed on the ground. We have already had a subliminal suggestion of his deed in "Leopold Bloom and the Nymph," as Bloom stands quiescent in the giant hand of the sensual goddess. In "Nausicaa," Bloom is similarly exposed to events, isolated as always, off to the side, all of his senses at work. Gerty herself, seen only in part—the vital part—is set off against a cold green background that suggests the sea lying beyond her and perhaps even the "cold and clammy" feeling that Bloom experiences as he walks off. In the engraving, her stockings—"Transparent stockings, stretched to breaking point"—are made of real mesh, and the black outlines of her legs have been rapidly sketched in order to suggest the spontaneity and speed of this encounter.

Around the characters are a related series of image: the fireworks along with the bat and the bicycle—drawn almost as if it, too, were flying—are found both in *Ulysses* and in a film that Field has made from the *Bloomsday Suite.* Each of these images is one of a kind, made just for the film and never pulled as an edition. As for the sketches with which the engraving began, they are an early attempt to isolate Bloom's senses, to chisel the event out from its narrative background and examine it in linear space. Done in four different media—pencil, india ink, ballpoint pen and felt-tip marker—they help to account for the finished sense of aloneness.

II

*Nausicaa
(Gerty MacDowell)*

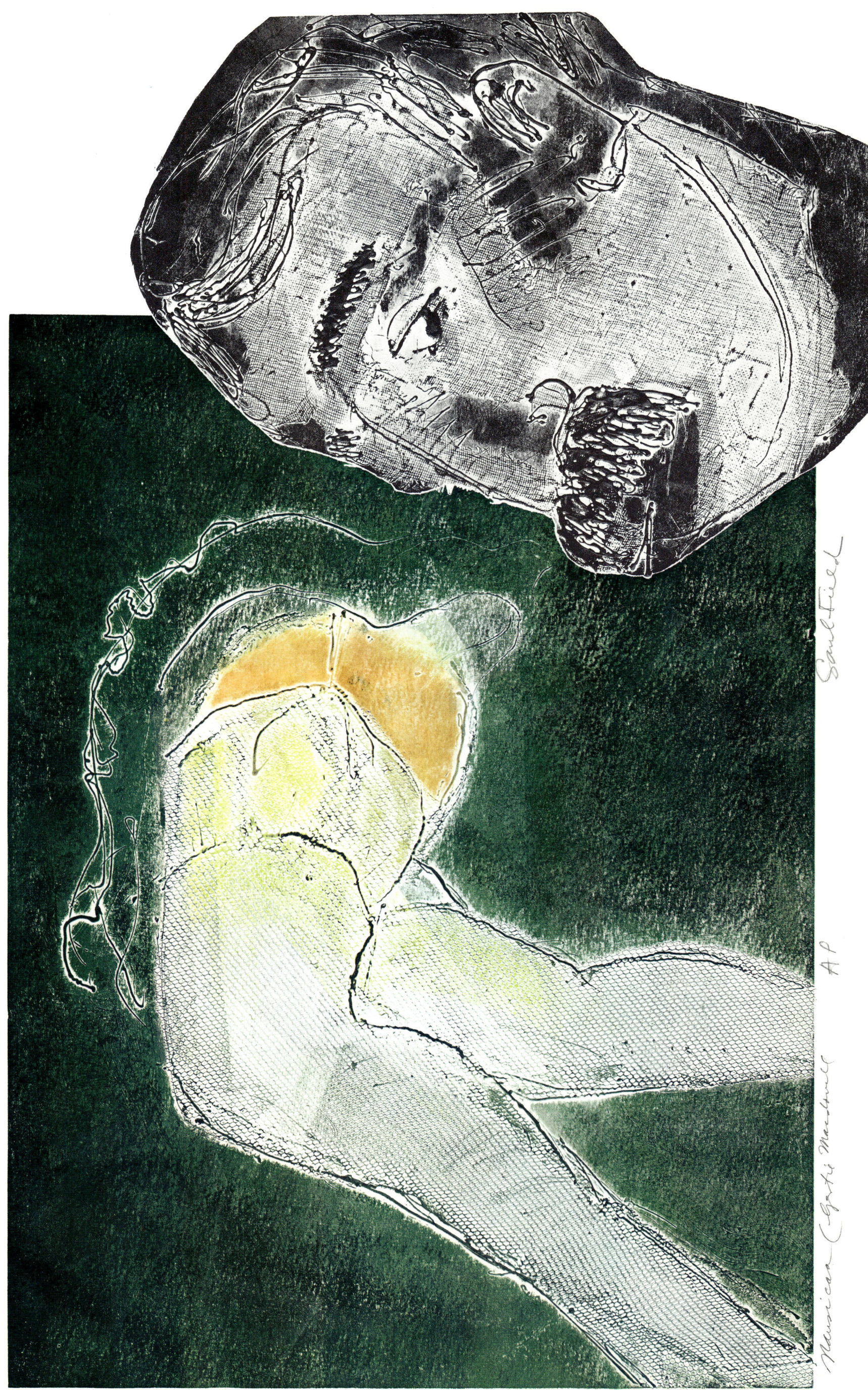

The Lying-in Hospital

"DESHIL HOLLES EAMUS" let us go south to Holles Street. Leopold and Molly used to live on this street, but the call now is to the lying-in hospital situated there. There Stephen and Bloom cross paths once again, this time not to part until the end of the day when they have made their spiritual communion. "Childe Leopold," knight errant of Dublin, has gone to the hospital to check on the progress of Mina Purefoy, a neighbor three days in labor and finally about to give birth. He finds there, unawares, memories of his own "manchild" heir dead long since at eleven days of age as well as the young man grown in body and mind but still immature as an artist who will serve as his surrogate son for the rest of this night and whom he will initiate mysteriously into artistic manhood.

"Oxen of the Sun"—named for the sacred herd of Apollo, god of light and of poetry—is in some ways the least successful chapter of the novel, the one in which Joyce's genius goes most nearly astray. Yet it provides the essential transition from the events of the day to the nighttime world of the final chapters—to Bella Cohen's whorehouse in Nighttown, to the cabman's shelter along the quays, to Eccles St. in the end. For it is now ten p.m., when June evenings in Dublin turn fully dark. Bloom on his mission of mercy comes upon Stephen who has had too much to drink and lost most of his money, whose friends are about to betray him—and follows him paternally to Nighttown.

This little action, however, is masked by the densest, the most difficult prose we have yet encountered, as Joyce parodies nearly all the masters of English style from the earliest writers in Anglo-Saxon and Anglo-Latin to the greatest Victorian essayists; in between, we may discover passages that seem to have come straight from *Everyman* and the *Morte d'Arthur*, from the King James Bible and Sir Thomas Browne, from *Piers Plowman*, Bunyan and Pepys, from Defoe, Swift, Addison and Steele, from Goldsmith, Sterne, Burke, Lamb, DeQuincey, Macaulay, Dickens, Pater, Newman, Carlyle and Burns, among others. The ingenuity of Joyce appears to be endless, and the recognition game, once we have learned the trick, is really great fun. But the fun quickly palls, and we become increasingly aware of the heavy hand of the creator: he should have been paring his fingernails indifferently, but he uses them instead to manipulate the strings of his puppets. If he differs from Thackeray at all in this chapter, it is only because his puppets are not characters but words. "Oxen of the Sun" is a magnificent tour de force, a feat unparalleled in the history of the language, but its very ingenuity nearly destroys the objectivity and distance that Joyce has so carefully wrought. Because it constantly reminds us of the presence of the author, its effects are ultimately negative, and we may doubt in the end that they were worth all the labor.

The scene of "The Lying-in Hospital," as Saul Field depicts it, occurs only in the imagination of Bloom: we never see the birth of Mrs. Purefoy's child. But a kind of symbolic birth does take place before our eyes, with Bloom the father and Stephen the son and the ghost of Rudy lurking somewhere beyond them. Thus the infant shown here is virtually interchangeable with the embryo of Rudy on page 35. In a psychological sense, it is also suggestive of Stephen, whom both Bloom and Molly recall as a child. Field has said of this engraving that he was trying to show science and humanity functioning together—a goal that Bloom himself would surely find admirable. But we must remember that Bloom as scientist, like Bloom as intellectual or Bloom as Jew, is invariably awry. What emerges from the print (even though he does not appear here in person), what emerges as well through the density of the prose, is Bloom the humanist: butt of the medical students' jokes, as out of place here as elsewhere in Dublin, more than just something of a schlemiel, he remains a man of compassion and decency. The men of Odysseus are destroyed in Homer for defiling the sacred herd of Apollo; the god of poetry in Joyce similarly destroys those who would defile Stephen and Bloom. The character of Bloom can survive even the occasional density of his creator.

The Lying-In Hospital

The Martello Tower

Paralleling Homer, Joyce also begins his epic with a son in search of his father, not some new protagonist but Stephen Dedalus, whom his readers would recall from *A Portrait of the Artist as a Young Man.* But there is a difference. The first four books of the *Odyssey*—the so-called Telemachia—relate the efforts of the Ithacan prince to locate his father and bring order and traditional values back to his homeland; in *Ulysses,* the first three chapters reveal Stephen attempting to complete the process of isolation begun in *A Portrait,* to free himself finally from the old ties of family, religion and nationality. Only when this process is complete can he find himself in his art, can he discover Bloom.

In both epics, however, these opening sections serve merely as prelude to the primary action, to the development of the true mythic hero as representative of his time: not the heir to the throne but his father, not Stephen but Bloom. The *Bloomsday Suite,* as its name implies, has a similar emphasis, so that Stephen and Molly appear as comparatively minor images in its perspective, as little more, in fact, than appendages of Bloom.

Thus we have altered the traditional narrative pattern and begun not with Stephen the seeker, but with Bloom, his ultimate goal. There are no images in the *Bloomsday Suite* of Stephen teaching history and math at Mr. Deasy's school in suburban Dalkey on Dublin Bay; or of Stephen walking along the beach on his way to town and working out in his mind a complex aesthetic—perhaps the first sustained example of stream of consciousness in modern literature; or, finally, of Stephen expounding to a band of hostile listeners in the National Library his imaginative yet ultimately absurd theory of the provenance of *Hamlet.* Even when his path crosses that of Bloom in the engravings, we see him, if at all, only through the eyes of his viewer. For this is truly Bloom's book and not Stephen's. We perceive this in the novel only toward the end. Because we do remember Stephen from *A Portrait* and because even *Ulysses* starts out as if it too were a traditional novel about the development of a sensitive, even artistic young man (a *Bildungsroman,* as it is known in the trade), we begin by expecting to identify with Stephen and only gradually discover that we are being led unto Bloom. It is middle-aged Bloom, hardly an artist in the usual sense of the term, nothing at all like the conventional heroes that we have learned to identify with— it is Bloom who dominates Stephen and gives him his meaning. Even Molly, who naturally has the last word, must ultimately be defined in terms of her husband.

This is not to imply, however, that Stephen is insignificant. Bloom may well give meaning to Stephen's life as an artist, but it is the artist who will immortalize Bloom; it is Stephen, we know, who will at the end of this day begin work on a strange new novel with the first anti-hero in modern literature, a novel suspiciously like the one that we call *Ulysses.* To a certain extent then, *Ulysses* is a novel concerned with its own creation, a reflexive work which cannot be read only once: for we must read through to the end to discover the kind of novel that Stephen will write.

This engraving shows Stephen at the Martello Tower with Buck Mulligan gesticulating at his side. Built originally against the threat of Napoleonic invasion, the chain of watchtowers along the coast had long been disused, except for occasional tenants like Stephen and Buck (or like Joyce and Oliver St. John Gogarty before them). Although we are told that it is Stephen who pays the rent for the tower, Mulligan eventually filches the key and dispossesses his roommate—one more step in the isolation of the artist, and not an entirely unwilling one at that. "A man of genius makes no mistakes," Stephen declares about Shakespeare. "His errors are volitional and are the portals of discovery." The incident, in any event, tells us something of Joyce's technique, for in real life—assuming that history is somehow more "real" than fiction—it was apparently Gogarty who paid the rent. The narrative change enlarges the sense of betrayal and the isolation which is its result. And Stephen's actions throughout this day seem designed to effect his complete isolation. Before it is over, he has given up his home, his job, his money and his friends. The process begun at the tower in "Telemachus," the opening chapter, is fulfilled at last in Holles Street and on the way to Nighttown. Here it is that he meets Bloom and finds more meaningful ties, a bond of the spirit.

Bloom and Stephen reach out to each other across the city, bridging the space and time that separate them. They are able to do so not only because Dublin is so small in area but also because of another modern perception that Joyce was one of the first to utilize in fiction: a new sense of the duration of time. This is the legacy of the French philosopher Henri Bergson, who taught us that it is wrong to consider time simply as an objective phenomenon, capable of being measured scientifically. Time, Bergson argued, is really subjective, a product of individual consciousness and not of the Greenwich Observatory. Thus, when we remember a series of past events, we do so not necessarily in the order in which they occurred, but as they occur to us now in memory, according to some inner connection and logic. Moreover, these events exist not only in the past but as they interact now with the present, as part of the present, simultaneously with it. In "Proteus"—named for the sea deity of infinite guises who gives us our word "protean"—Stephen walks along the seashore and considers the unities of space and of time: *nacheinander,* events occurring one after another, in the traditional sequence of time; and *nebeneinander,* things happening alongside one another, simultaneously. "A very short space of time through very short times of space."

The effect of all this on contemporary literature has been truly momentous. No longer do we need to interrupt the narrative flow in order to flash back to earlier events or other places; we can now show action occurring in both places at once, for the time is the same even if the settings are not. The Victorian novelist was forced to display time chronologically with past, present and future occurring in that general order and with no real way of dramatizing the effect of the past on the present or the likely effect of present events on the future. He could tell us omnisciently that there was—or would be—such an effect but he could not show it convincingly. And he was largely compelled to construct novels with a clearly delineated beginning, middle and end and to conclude each of his works definitively so that the action was complete for all time. Hence the pretty pink bow of a final chapter with which Dickens ties everything together and brings his readers up to date on the afterlife of each of his characters. Victorian omniscience and the traditional handling of time were obviously aspects of the same attitude toward life.

Modern novels, however, are likely to reflect our own sense of ambiguousness and to be open-ended instead. As a result, we discard not only the idealized Dickensian future existing outside the novel but any definite conclusion to the action at hand: Will the characters of *V.* by Thomas Pynchon ever discover their goal? Will the protagonist of *The Tin Drum* by Gunter Grass go out into the world and become the new savior? Will Robbe-Grillet's voyeur strike again? Time in modern fiction has become a major theme as well as a narrative device, and writers as disparate as Faulkner and Proust, Claude Simon and Carlos Fuentes, have dramatized its influence on the consciousness of individual men. "History," says Stephen Dedalus, late teacher of history, "is a nightmare from which I am trying to awake."

Time in *Ulysses* functions on several levels at once: as a force of history condemning Stephen and Bloom to their respective cultures; as that sense of memory which ties each man to his own particular past (Stephen to the deathbed scene of his mother, Bloom to the suicide of his father and the death of his son); and, finally, as simultaneity. In different parts of the city, in chapters separated by dozens of pages, Bloom and Stephen hear the sound of church bells or watch a ship sailing into the harbor or follow the lord mayor's parade, and we realize as they cannot that they are acting together, that already there is a bond between them that they cannot yet imagine.

Number 7 Eccles St. is miles from the Martello Tower but Stephen and Bloom rise to face the world at the same hour, and it is the same world that they face. The bonds between them were forged long before their inevitable meeting.

*Stephen at the
Martello Tower*

Ulysses, Joyce and Field in Nighttown

As Saul Field perceives it, the most dramatic scene in all of *Ulysses*—the one most realizable, that is, in visual terms—is "Circe," named for the goddess whose spell turns men into swine. In such chapters as "Proteus" and "Ithaca," the action is so internalized, so basically undramatic, that he devotes no graphics at all to them. But for "Circe," the longest chapter by far in the novel, with its rare blend of interior and exterior action, he has created five major prints and some subsidiary images as well. It was this mingling of outward event and inward reaction, this sense of the individual consciousness at odds with its environment, that lured Field to "Circe," and the graphic means he has devised for it are as imaginative and effective as Joyce's own innovations.

The technique of "Circe" is stream of consciousness, the best known yet least understood of Joycean modes. The term has come to be used so generally, in fact, and with so little sense of its particular context that it has lost virtually all of its original meaning and become another of those critical clichés. "Symbolism" is probably the only other literary term so widely misused. Writers of book reviews and of bookjacket blurbs, undergraduate students and occasionally even reputable scholars have used the term to refer broadly to any kind of internal action, as a synonym for "interior monologue." Part of the confusion arises from a misapplication of the French term *monologue intérieur*, which refers more to a particular technique of stream of consciousness than to the general sense of a character speaking to himself. In actuality, however, it is only one type of interior monologue, the very specialized development that is at work when a character interacts with the world around him and records unselfconsciously in his mind both his physical perceptions and the mental responses which they evoke, with none of the artificial order and logic that we impose on our conscious patterns of speech. Stream of consciousness (as both narrative device and psychological state) is thus somewhere between totally aware articulation and the hidden meanderings and meanings of the subconscious mind; it is a flowing, continuous movement, providing not so much a precise record of the mind at work as a sense of its workings, not each word and visualization but a poetic recreation of our mental processes as they function most of the time. We see it all as Bloom walks across the river toward Grafton Street:

Before the huge high door of the Irish house of parliament a flock of pigeons flew. Their little frolic after meals. Who will we do it on? I pick the fellow in black. Here goes. Here's good luck. Must be thrilling from the air. Apjohn, myself and Owen Goldberg up in the trees near Goose green playing the monkeys. Mackerel they called me.
A squad of constables debouched from College street, marching in Indian file....A squad of others...making for the station....
...
His smile faded as he walked, a heavy cloud hiding the sun slowly, shadowing Trinity's surly front. Trams passed one another, ingoing, outgoing, clanging. Useless words. Things go on same; day after day; squads of police marching out, back: trams in, out. Those two loonies mooching about. Dignam carted off. Mina Purefoy swollen belly on a bed groaning to have a child tugged out of her. One born every second somewhere. Other dying every second. Since I fed the birds five minutes. Three hundred kicked the bucket. Other three hundred born....
Cityful passing away, other cityful coming, passing away too: other coming on, passing on....
No one is anything.
This is the very worst hour of the day....

Bella Cohen (Circe)

Bloom is hungry and tired and perhaps this accounts for the tone of his thoughts. But we can see how they develop: from observation of his physical surroundings to memories of his youth and thoughts of his friends and finally to generalizations on human mortality. We also see something of his wit and his ability to identify with his surroundings. The policemen lead him by a kind of free association to a riot he once blundered into at Trinity College and to the medical students he encountered there. Later in the day, he will meet some of those students again, and they will lead him, perhaps inexorably, again to the police. "Wheels within wheels," Mr. Bloom is fond of recalling. Stream of consciousness, as Joyce uses it, is obviously more than a narrative technique; it becomes in his hands a major aspect of theme, a way of looking at life itself.

Joyce did not invent stream of consciousness as he is often said to have done. Edouard Dujardin had used it before him in *Les Lauriers sont coupés*, which was written in 1887 and published in English as *We'll to the Woods No More*. Some literary historians have found prefigurings of it in the works of such writers as Dostoevsky in *The Brothers Karamazov* and Dickens in *The Mystery of Edwin Drood*. But it was Joyce who perfected the technique, Joyce who discovered how to use it thematically and to give the impression of the stream rather than each undifferentiated drop of experience. For unless it is used selectively, the method can be terribly tedious; this is the lesson of Dorothy Richardson's monumental *Pilgrimage* in which the novelist acts more as an historian of her protagonist's consciousness than as a selective guide to her thoughts and reactions. Joyce makes no effort to present to us each instant of Bloom's day along with each sight and sound that he encounters and each thought that they evoke. He is concerned not with the stream as a whole but with the impression of the stream; for this, paradoxically, is closer to reality as each one of us lives it.

It is a long way, in any event, from the original use of internal monologue, itself an inevitable development in the novelist's continuing effort to dramatize individual states of mind. "Julien *said to himself*, What do I

know of this woman's character?...Heaven knows how many lovers she's had!" This was the best that Stendhal could do in 1830 in *The Red and the Black*; he understood the psychological truths that he wished to reveal, but he lacked the narrative tools to portray them. Major steps in the revolution in point of view since that time—milestones on the road to James Joyce—include the subtle renderings of Gustave Flaubert in *Madame Bovary* and Henry James in *The Spoils of Poynton*. This is Emma Bovary brooding over her husband's failure:

> *It was for him that she had done it—for this creature here, this man who understood nothing, who felt nothing. He was sitting quite calmly, utterly oblivious of the fact that the ridicule henceforth inseparable from his name would disgrace her as well. And she had tried to love him!*

And here is what Henry James called the central intelligence of the "other woman," Fleda Vetch, seen in a moral dilemma:

> *...she privately reflected that they were taking a great deal for granted, and that, inasmuch as to her knowledge Owen Gereth had positively denied his betrothal, the ground of their speculations was by no means firm. It seemed to our young lady that in a difficult position Owen conducted himself with some natural art....*

But Flaubert lapses at times into omniscience, and we are always aware of James peering over his characters' shoulders. Joyce learned from them and gave us Bloom, complete, without outside intervention, his own man on his own day.

Saul Field's effort throughout the *Bloomsday Suite* has been to develop graphic tools which can relate Joyce's insights in visual terms. Nowhere is this more apparent than in the engravings devoted to "Circe" and its stream of consciousness. We find here figures that are almost hard-edged yet at the same time blurred; the familiar tarleton cloth, burnt now as well as torn; plates used both as positive and as negative images; the face of Bloom looking somehow different and the face of Stephen virtually unrecognizable; other characters changing before our eyes from clear-cut naturalistic representations to wraith-like figures, barely identifiable as people; familiar objects strangely inverted—the bowl of a hat become a setting for action; handprints, fishnet stockings, sperm-like droppings of Field's drawing medium compotina, childish lettering on erotic pictures. These are the images of Bloom's hallucination, deeply compelling and wonderfully ironic, revelatory of his character and of Stephen's as well, going to the heart of the novel in its most spectacular episode. Few artists working in any medium have so ably captured the meaning and spirit of Joyce.

Abandoned by all of his friends except Lynch, on whom he had tried out his aesthetic theory in *A Portrait*, Stephen heads as if driven to Nighttown, the red-light district of Dublin. Here, Lynch too will finally desert him, and Stephen will be free at last of all the ties and encumbrances of his past. Now he is ready to encounter Bloom. The historical name for this district was Monto; if it no longer exists in physical fact—torn down by the city fathers in the interests of good citizenship—it has been immortalized, as renamed, in the novel.

Bloom has followed Stephen from the lying-in hospital to Nighttown for some unspecified reason: "What am I following him for?" he wonders. "Still, he's the best of that lot....Kismet." Perhaps because he has already begun to identify Stephen with Rudy he follows him here to watch over him. During the next few hours, in any event, he is fated to look after the young man's remaining possessions, to save him from a serious beating and from the police, to feed him and sober him up, to bring him home to Eccles St. and to offer him, unawares, a vision of life and of literature that few young artists had previously known. Their meeting takes place at Mrs. Bella Cohen's, number 82 Tyrone Street lower, not some cheap whorehouse but a place of distinction—"It's ten shillings here," the madam proclaims. The scene that follows, rendered in dramatic format, closely parallels the *Walpurgisnacht* episode in Goethe's *Faust,* a kind of black mass in which the sins of the hero are brought back to him.

The effect is nightmarish, as dream and reality fuse and blur, so that it becomes impossible to tell for certain where one ends and the other begins; the two forms of reality become as one, the inward vision intruding as much into external events as physical acts do into the world of dreams. Each time we think that the vision has ended and that we are back again in the conscious world, some dreamlike image appears and again blurs the distinction. In this state between waking and dreaming, which Freud labeled the preconscious state, we may well believe that we are fully awake when in fact we have already begun to yield to the logic of dreams. And Stephen has had far too much to drink; Bloom is tired and just a bit woozy, and in their streams of consciousness appear the characters and images that have obsessed them throughout the day, throughout their lives.

The Ten Shilling House

The hallucinatory feeling of the Nighttown engravings is captured in "The Ten Shilling House." Envisioned here are Bella Cohen off to the left, the weary and haunted face of Bloom the voyeur and the symbolic sisters of the prostitute Zoe, Kitty and Florry, apparitions as well as ten-shilling whores. Aside from Stephen, these are the only characters who function on both levels of action in the episode. The setting is the inverted bowler of Bloom, who is both witness to and silent participant in the Nighttown scenes: within this hat, in Saul Field's vision of "Circe," we find the symbolic burden of the entire chapter, the imaginative recreation of the nightmare spirit of the Nighttown events. The burned fringes of tarleton seem especially appropriate as the symbolic borderline of these events.

For us, it may be most intriguing to trace the visual progression of bowler-house and wraith-like whores, of erotic Bloom turning to guilt-ridden Bloom, for the artistic movement strangely parallels that of Bloom's own stream of consciousness.

The beginning for Field was simple enough, with the face of Bloom as it appears in an early black and white sketch (III). Then he produced the original page of drawings (opposite) which led both to "Bella-Bello" and to "The Ten Shilling House." We can follow the different directions that the artist took in the adjacent sketches numbered IV, for "Bella-Bello," and V, VI, and VII for the "House"; in the latter, for the first time, the hat is turned upside down. Shown on page 68 are the final preliminary sketch (VIII) for "The Ten Shilling House" and the two full-scale drawings (IX and X) from which Field eventually chose. In them we see the changing guises of the whores and the eerie glow of the Tiffany lamp under which they appear.

In this same series of drawings, we can also discover the origins of other erotic *Bloomsday* engravings: the first view of Gerty MacDowell (page 67, XI), the first impression of Hades (page 67, XII) and the primary sketches of what would become perhaps the most erotic and comic of all the prints, "Molly and Poldy" (page 68, XIII and XIV). Further steps in its development appear immediately below. This blend of erotic and comic links further the visions of Field, Joyce and even Leopold Bloom. It is hardly a characteristic common to western sensibility, but we find it in some of our greatest literary creations—in Falstaff and the Wife of Bath —as well as in the works of Picasso. In each case, paradoxically, we may detect just beneath the surface a potential dimension of tragedy.

III

The Ten Shilling House

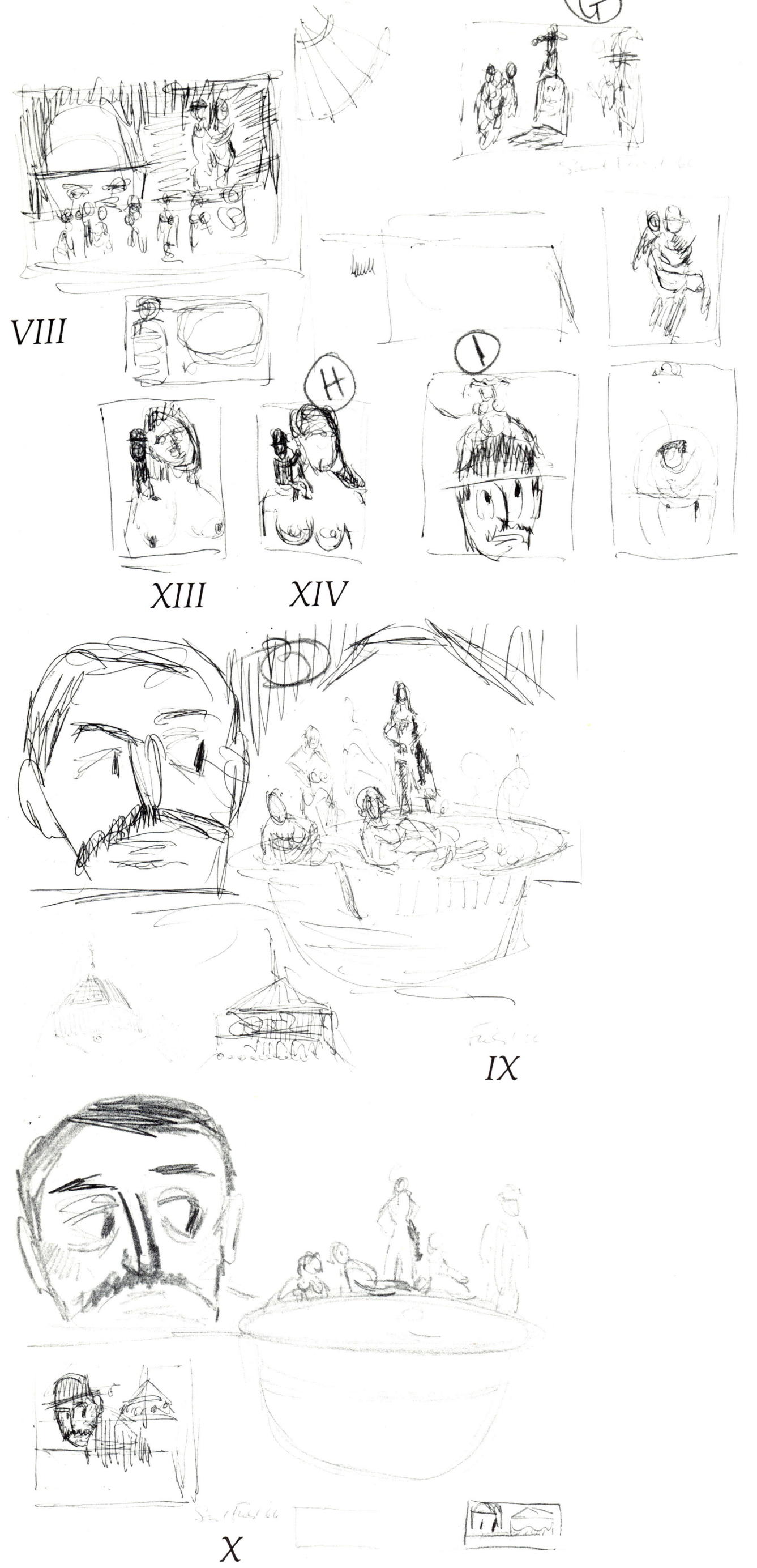

VIII

XIII XIV

IX

X

The Ten Shilling Horse
Artist's Proof

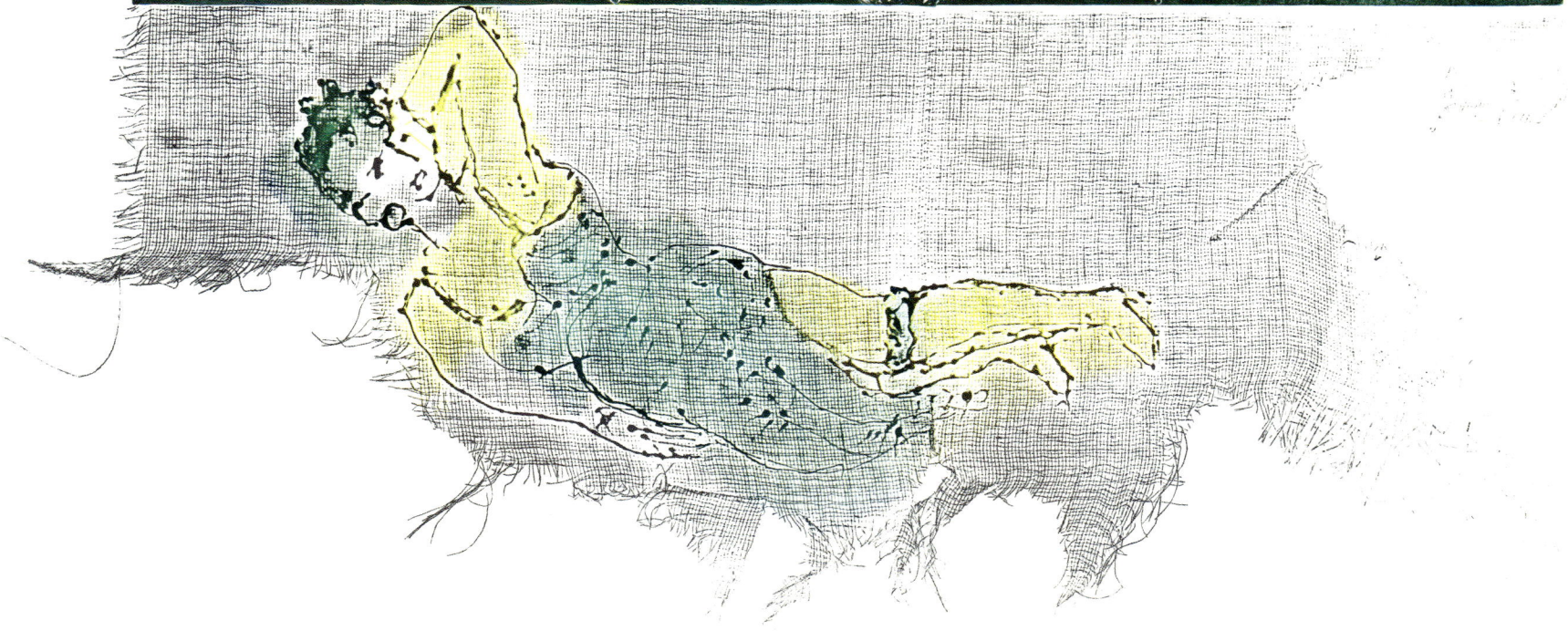

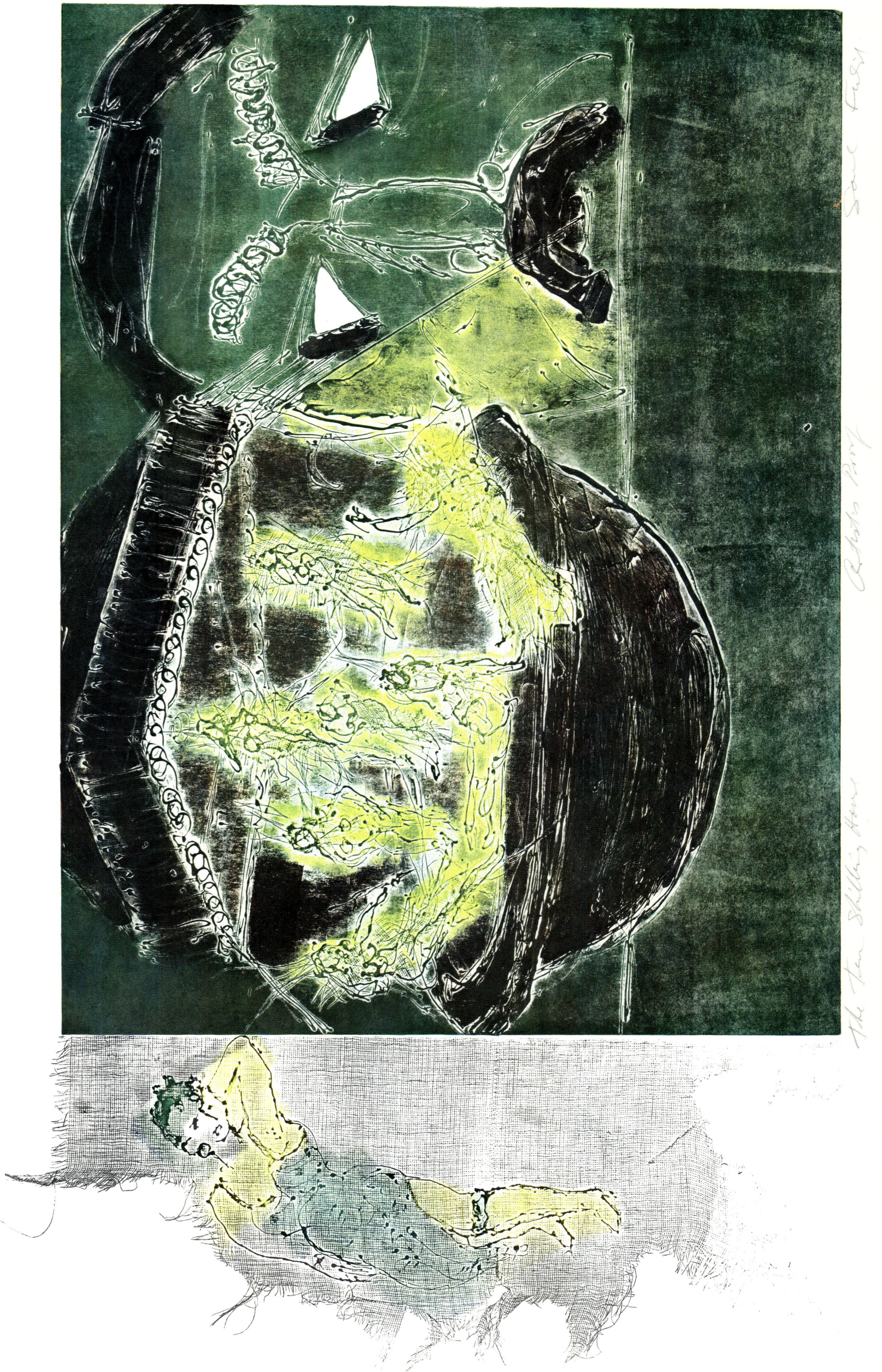

The Scullery Maid

In Nighttown, the hallucinatory trial scene begins with Mary Driscoll, "The Scullery Maid," accusing her former employer of terrible crimes. "He surprised me in the rere of the premises," she complains to the fantasy court. "He held me and I was discoloured in four places as a result. And he interfered twict with my clothing." As Bloom pleads his innocence, the complainant turns before his eyes into other women whom he has desired, not mere serving girls now but eminent ladies. There is no real evidence that Bloom has interfered with any of his alleged victims but in his guilt-ridden state there is no real need for evidence. "When in doubt," proclaims the culprit's attorney, "persecute Bloom."
Still another change takes place as Bloom, again without warning, becomes himself the savior of Ireland, the new Parnell, messiah to the Jews and Irish alike of "green Erin, the promised land of our common ancestors." Even the citizen, brushing aside a tear, blesses the new Irish leader. But in daydream as in history, the mob turns on Bloom-Parnell: "Fellowchristians and antiBloomites, the man called Bloom is from the roots of hell, a disgrace to christian men." In the eyes of the puritanical mob, even his religious and political sins appear to have sexual roots, and Bloom like Parnell before him is condemned as a "stinking goat," a "fiendish libertine from his earliest years." He has left his handprint behind as a sign of his complicity.
The scullery maid points the way to his sins, but Bloom, ever consistent, undresses her with his eyes even as she stands in the dock accusing him.

Mary Driscoll—
Scullery Maid

XV

72

14

Bella-Bello

Here she is, ladies and gents, Mrs. Bella Cohen, riding postilion to Leopold Bloom, onetime savior of his nation, longtime holder of masochistic desires. "The lady goes a pace a pace and the coachman goes a trot a trot and the gentleman goes a gallop a gallop a gallop a gallop."
But this is no real cockhorse that she rides. This is the famed "Adorer of the adulterous rump!" Because the dream references of "Circe" work forward as well as backward in time, we will not discover until much later what this sobriquet means. We have long noticed Bloom's feminine tendencies. Who else would experience sympathetic labor pains for an acquaintance? And we have observed from early morning his liking for beefy, powerful women—women, we now understand, who might dominate him. So it seems quite natural to move from the accusations of the scullery maid to this masochistic, transvestite orgy, as Bloom and Bella change not merely clothes but identities: Bella the madam becomes Bello the dominating man, and Bloom in a sense becomes both, both woman and man, both victim and torturer, in himself the Shakespearean beast with two backs—and two fronts as well.
This bisexuality is perhaps the best account in modern fiction of what we are inclined to label abnormal behavior, a serious subject indeed. Yet as we study Saul Field's visualization of this scene, we also recognize that it is inherently funny, and we remember again that *Ulysses* is a great comic novel, that in its ironic worldview even the most tragic possibilities will soon be undercut by the comic.
"Master!" Bloom calls out to Bello. "Mistress!" he cries. "Mantamer!... I have sinned! I have suff...," and then he dies. But before we have time to be affected by his condition, he crawls out from under the boughs which shelter his corpse and is immediately confronted by the nymph whose portrait hangs over his bed: "What have I not seen in that chamber?" she mourns. "What must my eyes look down on?" And Bloom, who just a moment before perished as a result of his guilt, now apologizes self-consciously for the dirty linen that fills his bedroom and for the

cracked commode. Somehow we are moved even as we laugh at him, for his is an unpredictable, inconsistent, ever-changing, marvelous vision of the realities of dream.

Field's own path to this vision began with various sketches of Bloom abject—with his hat in his hand and down on his knees. Then he moved on to an experiment in design, with "Bella-Bello" pictured from both positive and negative points of view. It was the negative design (top right, XVIII) which won out. On the finished print we also notice the drops of sperm that surround the two-headed figure (the compotina compound squirted from a hypodermic needle); the real fishnet stockings that Bella wears and the web of tarleton that tears off from them and her gloves; the ironic shamrocks that float in the air as a sign of Irish nationalism in Nighttown; and the unconsecutive text, lettered initially by the artist's young daughter and then engraved by him on the plate. What emerges is a solid reality, yet at the same time everything appears somewhat dreamlike, partly disembodied like Bella.

Bella-Bello

XVI

XVII   XVIII

"My Girl's a Yorkshire Girl"

Stephen, meanwhile, is caught up in his own nightmare scene. Hard-faced and silent in the spectral setting, he sits at the piano playing a series of "empty fifths," and Bloom, listening outside (for we are back again at the start of the episode), hears what seems to be church music and enters to find Stephen within. Soon Zoe will start up the two-penny pianola. Lights flashing, in waltz time, it gives forth that famous old tune, "My Girl's a Yorkshire Girl, Yorkshire through and through"—and Stephen will dance madly around the room first with her and then with Florry and Kitty.

> *Two young fellows were talking about their girls, girls, girls,*
> *Sweethearts they'd left behind....*

And then, suddenly, his dead mother appears.

It is almost impossible at this point to distinguish between physical action and dream—to separate the dead from the dance—or even to tell for certain whose dream it is that we are involved in. In this respect, the atmosphere of "Circe" foreshadows the later *Finnegans Wake*, which is concerned with the night as *Ulysses* is with the day. The language of the *Wake* is throughout the language of dream, and although there may well be many dreamers, it is a single, universal dream that they share. In "Circe," Stephen's hallucination now overlaps Bloom's, and it becomes apparent at last that each man's guilt is akin to the other's.

In order to suggest the simultaneity of the Joycean episode, Field condenses the action in the engraving so that Stephen appears in several guises at once—at the piano, dancing with one of the girls, perhaps even as a spectator at the rear. But this is not quite the same Stephen whom we saw earlier at the Martello Tower. He seems older and harder at the end of the day and also, as we will soon see for ourselves, more susceptible to the guilt that enfolds him. If he is less individualized in appearance than either Bloom or Molly, it is because Field sees him as a more universalized character, as almost a cliché of the developing young artist. He is both less and more than they are: less, because he is hardly as memorable; more, because he is the one who will ultimately immortalize them. Now, however, he has only what he calls his "Dance of death."

My Girl's a Yorkshire Girl

Stephen's Mother and the Fox

In his dreams, each man's most dreaded desire seems to be realized: Bloom panders for Boylan, and Stephen's mother comes up from the dead.

When we left Stephen at the close of *A Portrait of the Artist as a Young Man*, he was preparing to leave Ireland for Paris, there to continue the ritual of dedication to his art and separation from his past. (As Joyce himself pronounced the title of his first finished novel, the emphasis was on the final phrase: Stephen is not yet an artist; he is merely a young man who may someday become one.) We may thus be surprised to find him again in Dublin at the start of *Ulysses.* We soon learn the reason for his return—a simple telegram: "Mother dying come home father"— but not until "Circe" do we ascertain its effect on his life.

"O, it's only Dedalus," Buck Mulligan has said, "whose mother is beastly dead." Mulligan has handled too many cadavers in anatomy class to have much concern for the dead and, besides, this is an age of science and disrespect for the old verities. Stephen purports to be angered, however, not at the slight to his mother but at the offense to himself. To Mulligan, this is just one more example of his roommate's perversity but Stephen cannot disguise his anxiety from us. Out of a sense of intellectual integrity, he has refused his mother's last wish to pray at her deathbed. He says in *A Portrait,* "I will not serve that in which I no longer believe." As he once objected to making his Easter duty in order to please his mother while she was alive, so now he will not pray for her at the moment of death: he does his duty now through his guilt.

Joyce expresses this guilt indirectly, through a cluster of images which appear individually throughout the novel and coalesce finally in Nighttown: the smell of rosewood and ashes in the mother's graveclothes; the churchbells ringing out the prayer for the dead, *Liliata rutilantium...*; the fox which Stephen associates with her and with himself. On the morning of June 16, he has asked his students an old folk riddle, strangely suggesting death and rebirth. Its answer is "The fox burying his grandmother under a hollybush." And Stephen imagines: "A poor soul gone to heaven: and on a heath beneath winking stars a fox, red reek of rapine in his fur, with merciless bright eyes scraped in the earth, listened, scraped up the earth, listened, scraped and scraped." Later that night, the fox appears to Stephen at Bella Cohen's, and he thinks: "Thirsty fox. ...Burying his grandmother. Probably he killed her." And then in an instant appears the spectre of his mother, graveclothes faded and torn, "her face worn and noseless, green with grave mould." Behind her, a choir of virgins sings out the deathbed prayer and Stephen for the first time confronts the roots of his guilt. It is his most abject moment of the day, yet strangely enough it is the beginning of his freedom.

Stephen's Mother

The Fox

The Ashplant

The apparition of May Goulding Dedalus calls out in death as in life to her firstborn son: "I pray for you in my other world....Save him from hell, O divine Sacred Heart!...Have mercy on Stephen, Lord, for my sake! Inexpressible was my anguish when expiring with love, grief and agony on Mount Calvary." Some of these words are certainly hers; her son must have heard them so often that he knows them by heart. But others can only be his; they are too balanced, too intellectualized and self-conscious to have come from anyone but the would-be young artist. To some extent then, he is heightening the effect of his mother's terrible words by adding to them his own. Thus he exercises some control over this spectre even as it torments him. In this dance of death, as he does with the fox, Stephen plays dual dramatic roles—both parent and son, the quick and the dead, a character in art and its creator. Even in his anguish, he retains his sense of artistic creation. Ironically, some ultimate creator is structuring this same experience in ways unknown even to him. That first phrase that Mrs. Dedalus speaks has its own echoes in the consciousness of Bloom—of all people—for he too thinks at various points during the day about that same "other world." Neither is aware of it but this is actually the first communion between Stephen and Bloom. "They said I killed you, mother. He offended your memory. Cancer did it, not I..Destiny." But she will not be assuaged so easily and so, in desperation, in an effort to shatter her image, he swings his ashplant at the chandelier over his head: glass splinters down, the flame of time, "ruin of all space." The image vanishes, the nightmare is over, he abandons his ashplant and rushes out into the street.

Stephen and the Ashplant

Cissy Caffrey

Out in the street again, Stephen runs unerringly—almost willfully—into yet another difficulty. This time, it involves an old acquaintance of ours, Miss Cissy Caffrey, and some representatives of the imperial forces in Ireland.

When Gerty MacDowell walked earlier along Sandymount strand, she was accompanied by her friend Cissy Caffrey, acting as nursemaid to her two small brothers. "None of your spoilt beauties" is this young maiden, but "a girl lovable in the extreme," albeit "a forward piece whenever she thought she had a good opportunity to show off...her skinny shanks...." Bloom sees her again at the entrance to Nighttown in the company of two English soldiers, Private Compton and Carr. (Their names are apparently derived from two British consular officials in Zurich during Joyce's first tenure there and the incident itself from his first day in Trieste—another example of his willingness to use any material at hand, no matter how slight.) Now, rushing into Tyrone street, Stephen lurches drunkenly into their midst. Private Carr acts as cavalier to his lady: "Was he insulting you?"

CISSY: *...I'm faithful to the man that's treating me though I'm only a shilling whore.*
PRIVATE COMPTON: *Biff him one, Harry.*
PRIVATE CARR: *Say, how would it be, governor, if I was to bash in your jaw?*
STEPHEN: *Struggle for life is the law of existence, but modern philirenists notably the tsar and the king of England, have invented arbitration. (He taps his brow.) But in here it is I must kill the priest and the king.*
PRIVATE CARR: *What's that you're saying about my king?*
BLOOM: *He doesn't know what he's saying. Taking a little more than is good for him....I know him. He's a gentleman, a poet.*
PRIVATE CARR: *I don't give a bugger who he is.*
PRIVATE COMPTON: *We don't give a bugger who he is.*

> BLOOM: *(To Stephen.) Come home. You'll get into trouble.*
> PRIVATE CARR: *(Tugging at his belt.) I'll wring the neck of any bugger says a word against my fucking king.*
> CISSY: *They're going to fight. For me.*
> BLOOM: *(Shakes Cissy Caffrey's shoulders.) Speak, you! Are you struck dumb? You are the link between nations and generations. Speak, woman, sacred lifegiver!*
> CISSY: *(Alarmed, seizes Private Carr's sleeve.) Amn't I with you? Amn't I your girl? Cissy's your girl. (She cries.) Police!*

Cissy Caffrey

The spectators cry out. Brimstone fires blaze up in the background. "The midnight sun is darkened. The earth trembles." Private Carr knocks Stephen to the ground, and Lynch, who has been silently watching with Kitty, walks back now into the house with her. The last link to the old life is gone. It is Bloom who will raise Stephen as from the dead, who will lift him up from the ground, shelter and feed him, bring him new life back home in Eccles St. As he looks now at the silent form lying before him, Bloom experiences his own final vision: "a fairy boy of eleven, a changeling, kidnapped,... holding a book in his hand. He reads from right to left inaudibly, smiling, kissing the page.

> BLOOM: *(Wonderstruck, calls inaudibly.) Rudy!*

The union is complete, the nightmare concluded. Regeneration is about to begin.

Eumaeus the Swineherd and the Cabman's Shelter

"Hardly a stonesthrow away" from Mabbott Street, in the vicinity of the Liffey embankment close by the Butt Bridge, stands the cabman's shelter, run by a once-famous revolutionary known as Skin-the-Goat. It is here that Bloom, "in orthodox Samaritan fashion," leads his weary young friend.

They have finally made contact and over coffee they speak at last of the subjects nearest to each of their hearts: history and literature, Ireland and the Jews. We have seen signs throughout the day of their impending spiritual union, yet now, ironically, they disagree on everything they discuss. As the narrative puts it, "the views of the pair, poles apart as they were, both in schooling and everything else, with the marked difference in their respective ages, clashed." The desultory language is Bloom's, reflecting his own tired state. Perhaps it is simply too late in the day for them to be joined; this may be just one more of those unfortunate missed connections that seem to dominate their lives.

But something does happen to Stephen. Perhaps because he has been shown a picture of Molly, perhaps because he has perceived something in Bloom: in any event, he agrees to follow his savior to Eccles St. Their path will take them along the Liffey, the river that runs through the center of Dublin, the major symbol of *Finnegans Wake* and even here a sign of the spiritual rebirth about to take place. The bridge and the church [Adam and Eve's Church] whose bells mark the hour of the day mark their way homeward to number 7.

Adam and Eve's Church

Butt Bridge

Bloom, like Stephen, is keyless at the end of the day, and so he must leap over the railing and enter his home through the basement. Even this spectacular opening seems mundane and matter-of-fact, however, in the question and answer format of "Ithaca," a style reminiscent of certain textbooks of the time. The point of view again is Bloom's, but the results somehow are different from before:

> *Did Bloom discover common factors of similarity between their respective like and unlike reactions to experience? Both were sensitive to artistic impressions musical in preference to plastic or pictorial. Both preferred a continental to an insular manner of life.... Both indurated by early domestic training and an inherited tenacity of heterodox resistance professed their disbelief in many orthodox...doctrines.*

Enjoying the Homeric hospitality of the Blooms' kitchen, Stephen again speaks with his host of religion and family, of literature and art, of nationality and the universe. And now they find much to agree upon. Finally, Bloom suggests to Stephen that the guest may wish to stay on, at least for a time (to teach Molly Italian perhaps, perhaps to supplant Boylan in her affections).

> *Was the proposal of asylum accepted? Promptly, inexplicably, with amicability, gratefully it was declined.*

Because we do not see things from Stephen's viewpoint during these final chapters, we can only guess at the reasons for his refusal and the effect of this encounter on his life and his art. However, we may suspect that he too has been moved by Bloom, that he has found at the end of this fateful day a meaningful bond to replace those he earlier discarded. Wherever he goes after he leaves Eccles St., surely he has become an artist at last.

Home Again Now in Ithaca

Bloom is the metaphor for which he has been searching: "As a competent keyless citizen he [has] proceeded," like Bloom, "from the unknown to the known through the incertitude of the void."

As Stephen departs, guest and host walk into the yard and in a kind of fertility paean urinate together under the window of the moon goddess herself, celebrating her life-giving forces: "her power to enamour, to mortify, to invest with beauty, to render insane...the tranquil inscrutability of her visage...her splendor, when visible: her attraction, when invisible." Again the bells ring and Stephen goes off into the moon-filled night.

Alone once again, Bloom makes up the balance sheet of his day's activities, glances over his library, rummages carefully through the artifacts of his life. In the first drawer of his desk, he finds old lottery tickets and postage stamps, an exercise chart with periodic notations, young Milly's copybook with several drawings, a prospectus for Wonderworker, "the world's greatest remedy for rectal complaints," two obscene photographs and four letters sent secretly by Martha Clifford of Dolphin's Barn. In the second drawer: an ancient Passover hagadah, an "indistinct daguerreotype of Rudolph Virag [Bloom] and his father Leopold Virag executed in the year 1852," an envelope addressed *To my Dear Son Leopold.* For the first time we see his father's suicide note: widowed, ailing, a septuagenarian, he has taken poison, asking only kindness for his dog and to be remembered by his son. On the twenty-seventh of this month, Leopold will travel to Ennis to observe the anniversary of his father's death, but it is clear that he has been mourning him throughout this day, through much of his life. And with him he mourns his own dead son, the ethnic deadend of Rudolph and Leopold and Rudy.

It was from old Rudolph Bloom, who converted to Christianity out of physical and not spiritual hunger, that Leopold received his Jewish inheritance. But because as a young man he resisted his father's orthodox teaching, his mature sense of his Jewishness is strangely distorted. Bap-

Metempsychosis

tized a Protestant at birth and again as a Catholic at the time of his marriage, he nonetheless thinks of Christians as "them," while they think of him as a Jew. Thus it is hardly surprising that there are so many Jewish references in *Ulysses* — more than two hundred in all, perhaps the most prevalent of its many motifs — or that each one of them is marked by some error or incompleteness. Bloom himself is unsure that he has the right to be labeled a Jew, yet this is the surest sign of his identity in this alien culture in which he has lived all of his life. The death of Rudy means that it must all end with him; yet Bloom perseveres. What has most pleased him about this day? he asks himself late in the night. "To have sustained no positive loss. To have brought a positive gain to others." In the words of the prophet known as Second Isaiah, "Light to the gentiles."

Joyce made his hero a Jew not simply because he saw similarities between the sufferings of the Irish and those of the Jews or even because Odysseus was an archetypal Wandering Jew. Nor was his choice arbitrary, as some readers have thought. Bloom is a Jew precisely because he is the representative man of our time; the Jew's experience in history predicts that of all men today. He is the first of the twentieth-century anti-heroes and he warns us not only that life for us has diminished but also that we may still persevere. Eternally victimized, yet forever persistent, he manages somehow to endure, to live in dignity and survive those who would destroy him. Bloom as cuckold is the victim of our crudest, most condescending remarks; as hero, however, he reminds us of our own morality and the possibility that we too may somehow transcend it. At a time when it was fashionable to deride the Jew as the cause of the modern predicament (witness Eliot and Pound), Joyce perceived that he was its foremost victim, as well as a symbol of the potential for continuity. It was an artistic decision, then, to make his hero a Jew but one clearly reflecting Joyce's own sympathies.

This is a heavy burden for poor Bloom to carry so late in the night. For now he is concerned not with the family of man but with his own family life. Slowly he rises, gathering his clothes; he walks up the stairs to the bedroom, climbs into bed, lies with his head to the feet of his still-awake wife. In silent adoration, he kisses the "plump mellow yellow smellow melons of her [adulterous] rump." Again, on the verge of sentiment, Joyce undercuts the heroic with the ironic. And, finally,

Womb? Weary?
He rests. He has travelled.

Metempsychosis A.P. Saul Field

21

With her husband asleep, Molly takes over as narrator in one of the most spectacular and controversial episodes in modern literature. Her closing soliloquy is sentimental and sensual, coarse and lyrical, a stream of consciousness summary of the day's activities and of much of her life as well. We discover in "Penelope" something of her attitudes toward sex, toward her husband, toward life as a whole, and we find more depth of feeling than we might have expected. For, surprisingly, there is ambiguity about her as well as her husband.

About sex, for example: "...why cant you kiss a man without going and marrying him first you sometimes love to wildly when you feel that way so nice all over you you cant help yourself...theres nothing like a kiss long and hot down to your soul almost paralyses you...." And yet she thinks, in apparent dissatisfaction, "nice invention they made for women for him to get all the pleasure." Her sex life with Bloom since the death of their son has left much to be desired, and he naturally assumes that she has had many lovers to fill the gap. Yet she seems to suggest that Boylan may be the first, or at least the first in some time, and we are tempted to sympathize with her predicament: "O thanks be to the great God I got somebody to give me what I badly wanted to put some heart up into me." There are even some areas in which she favors Bloom over Boylan. "Poldy," she informs us, "has more spunk in him."

There is much that she tells us about Leopold, in fact. She is scornful of his visionary projects to improve the quality of life, but she respects him as provider for his own family. She claims to be disinterested in his activi-

Penelope Discovered

ties, but she demonstrates concern—even a bit of jealousy—over his deeds on this day. She confirms his fetishism—"of course hes mad on the subject of drawers." She wonders why he has brought Stephen home, thinks of the young man as a potential lover and, like her husband, identifies him with Rudy. She too, we learn, has suffered from the death of their child: "I suppose I oughtnt to have buried him in that little woolly jacket I knitted crying as I was but give it to some poor child but I knew well Id never have another our 1st death too it was we were never the same since O Im not going to think myself into the glooms about that any more...."

It is almost impossible to be objective about Molly. She offers herself so revealingly, so intimately, that we know more about her than almost any character in literature. She is able to inspire some men to great deeds (figuratively), but she is also a narrow, self-indulgent housewife pre-occupied with her own petty affairs. In the ancient tradition of Moll Flanders and the Wife of Bath, she is both fertility goddess and slob. But because she is so honest about her concerns and because Poldy himself views her so lovingly, we are inclined to like her more, perhaps, than we thought we should. We are not moved by her as by Bloom but some part of us all responds to her vitality. Still, she is not the heart of the narrative. She is a marvelous figure, but her function is to lead us to Everyman-Bloom.

We get some sense of the complexity of Molly's relationship with Poldy from these final engravings from the *Bloomsday Suite,* vignettes of their emotional life together.

Blazes and Molly

This view of "Blazes and Molly" is again Leopold's, as he imagines the tryst between his wife and her lover, acting himself as procurer and onlooker. Begun as a series of naturalistic drawings (page 106, XIX), the finished work shows the female animal in all her fleshiness, as both Boylan and Bloom seem to prefer her. Her accoutrements confirm her appeal. Hanging from her outstretched right arm are the panties that Bloom carries with him during the day, a sign here of his vicarious involvement in her affair. Along her other arm are thick strands of tarleton that make her appear rather feline; they also suggest the consciousness of her particular viewer. Thus, as Bloom sees the lovers, Boylan the intruder is appropriately faceless, while Molly somehow emerges romantic and stylized.

Blazes Boylan and Molly

XIX

Molly's Soliloquy

Molly reappears in her soliloquy precisely as we first met her at "#7 Eccles St."—through some process of metempsychosis, no doubt. The two forms of her re-emergence are separate second generation images derived from the original. Within this single print (page 111) the negative image, on the left, is the direct pressing, without ink, from the original tarleton plate; the image on the right (both positive and negative) shows her encased in a form that seems to be both keyhole and phallus—appropriate symbols of her position in life. Together, they suggest Molly in the flesh and Molly in spirit, the two main guises in which her husband perceives her.

The voyeur, of course, is Bloom once again but it is also the reader, for we are the only true witnesses to her soliloquy. But questions arise that even we cannot answer. What precisely was the relationship between Bloom and the serving girl Mary Driscoll, whom Molly dismissed years before but whom she still remembers with anger? Is it in any way significant that Molly, like all the other major women of the novel, has her period on this particular day? How are we to interpret Bloom's suggestion that his wife bring him breakfast in bed in the morning? Some critics have viewed this request as a sign of a new regime in their household, perhaps of a revitalized sex life for them, possibly even a new male heir. This seems to be a great deal to infer from a desire for a couple of eggs, but we simply cannot be sure. For this is the account of one day only, and in this "chaffering all including most farraginous chronicle" anything seems possible. Molly's soliloquy, like the narrative as a whole, gives us a great deal of insight into a great many topics, but there is much that it pointedly omits, that we cannot quite comprehend. It is thus very much like life itself, a masterful blending of artistic form and philosophical content.

Molly's Soliloquy

Molly and Poldy

"...he said I was a flower of the mountain yes so we are flowers all a womans body yes...that was why I liked him because I saw he understood or felt what a woman is and I knew I could always get round him...." Bloom reads more than Molly, is more sensitive than she is, more experienced and capable, yet she dominates their relationship. In his mind's eye, he diminishes as she grows ever larger. The perspective of "Molly and Poldy" is his then but it coincides with her own. She is bejeweled and beautiful, an exotic goddess, while he is a small cartoon figure, almost a puppet, less individualized here than in any of his other appearances. For a time even, he becomes blurred with other men in her memory. As she drifts off into sleep, she confuses the men she has known—Boylan and Bloom and Lieutenant Mulvey ("what was his name Jack Joe Harry") who first kissed her when she was a girl in Gibraltar. But it is Bloom who is with her at the end.
In the early afternoon, Bloom has been stirred by the touch of the sun—"a secret touch telling me memory"—to recall the days of their courtship, lying together surrounded by flowers on the Hill of Howth, overlooking the bay and the city. He recalls the past with excitement, but ends in depression over the present:

> *Ravished over her I lay, full lips full open, kissed her mouth....Wildly I lay on her, kissed her....She kissed me. I was kissed. All yielding she tossed my hair. Kissed, she kissed me.*
> *Me. And me now.*

Her memory, however, is less ambiguous. She confuses Gibraltar and Dublin, but her sense of past joy is unaffected by thoughts of the present: "...the sun shines for you he said the day we were lying among the rhododendrons on Howth head...the day I got him to propose to me... I was thinking of so many things he didn't know of...the sentry in front of the governors house...and the Spanish girls laughing in their shawls

and their tall combs and the auctions in the morning the Greeks and the Jews and the Arabs…and those handsome Moors all in white… and Ronda with the old windows of the posadas…and Gibraltar as a girl where I was a Flower of the mountain yes…and then I asked him with my eyes to ask again yes and then he asked me would I yes to say yes my mountain flower and first I put my arms around him yes and drew him down to me so he could feel my breasts all perfume yes and his heart was going like mad and yes I said yes I will Yes."
Molly's soliloquy is an affirmation of the lyrical potential in human life, a paean to the physical senses and to the poetry implicit in each man's consciousness. Its lyricism flowers in the midst of pathos and humor, of low comedy and near tragedy. The *Bloomsday Suite* gives us that same sense of sorrow and joy, of the "me now" and the "Yes" and the ambiguity as well of the Blooms' relationship, and of all human life.
The novel ends dramatically with Molly, but it is Bloom who remains with us.
Bloom, the outsider, looks on life with curiosity, concern and affection, open to experience, eager to learn. He is the representative hero of a most unheroic era, but his quest for personal dignity lifts him above those around him. It may be foolish to seek meaning in a world so obviously lacking in meaning, but Bloom is ennobled by his search, as we ourselves would be. We do well to study him in this age of alienation: to know Bloom is to know ourselves.

Molly and Poldy

XX
Early Sketches for *Molly and Poldy*

Molly's Soliloquy
(detail)

Afterword

Early in 1971 Saul Field (at that time unknown to me) arrived at the Print Club wanting to show me his work. I was so impressed with the excellence and unique qualities of his prints that I quickly became interested both in them and their literary inspiration—indeed, I decided to give Field a one-man exhibition at the Club's galleries. When he and Morton Levitt told me of their plans for this book and asked me to write an afterword, I decided that the most appropriate area to cover would be Saul Field's method of printmaking, which embodies several innovative features.

Field's "compotina" technique derives largely from two twentieth century developments in the five hundred year old craft of intaglio printmaking. Traditionally, intaglio prints use metal plates which are etched or engraved with the print design. In printing, these plates are inked and then wiped so that the ink is retained in the incised grooves. A sheet of paper, dampened to increase its pliability, is placed in contact with the plate, covered with a blanket and passed between the rollers of a press under very strong pressure. The paper is deformed into the lowered, design areas of the plate, and the residual ink adheres, transferring the image onto the sheet.

The novel aspect of Saul Field's plates is that they are built up as a collage—using paper and other materials—and then hardened to withstand printing pressure. Field uses an acidless substance—compotina—invented and developed by himself and his wife, artist Jean Townsend. Compotina may be made in various consistencies, ranging from a paste to be applied with a spatula, to a fluid with which the artist can draw directly on the plate using a hypodermic needle. This latter use creates the very calligraphic line which characterizes Field's prints. The incorporation of many "found" materials, notably tarleton (a heavy-duty muslin long used by print makers for the wiping of the excess ink from the plates) and textured papers give the plates an extraordinary versatility. Furthermore, all these materials may be easily cut with scissors;

the coping saw used by traditional etchers has no place in Field's studio.

The "second generation" plates referred to in Morton Levitt's text are created in two ways. In the first, the cardboard support on which a tarleton plate is made receives the excess compotina, creating a new image that relates to the primary in both a positive and negative manner; the web of the tarleton leaves a negative impression as it is lifted off the support card and the compotina applied with the needle forms a positive "echo" image where it has passed through the cloth onto the cardboard below. In the second, a completed primary plate, such as the one used in "Metempsychosis" (page 101) is covered with a separation layer, placed in contact with a dried compotina-coated sheet of paper and passed through the press, creating a negative image on the secondary sheet. These two types of second generation plates appear together at the foot of "Molly's Soliloquy" (page 111).

In the printing of his plates, Saul Field uses both oil-base and water-base inks (metal plates would not accept the water-base ones). Different viscosities in the inks, coupled with the use of rollers of varying hardnesses which will penetrate different depths into the plate (Field uses rollers ranging from soft gelatine to marble), result in distinct areas of the image accepting different colored inks. In successive impressions this separation is very consistent, though every print shows slight variations. Thus, many colors can be applied to the plate at one time and transferred to the paper in one printing process, as in the print "Bella Cohen" (page 61). Because the plates are very thin, they can be laid on top of each other during the passage through the press without damaging the paper. The silhouette of Bloom in "Metempsychosis" (page 101) is an example of an overlaid plate.

All this technical innovation is part and parcel of Saul Field's repertoire of craftsmanship. He avoids the common pitfall of confusing technical mastery with artistic merit, but well recognizes that craftsmanship must remain subservient to strength of image. Approaches to literary illustration can be either literal, as in most children's books, or metaphorical, as here. Field's prints are never the exact translation of a verbal description into visual terms; rather they tend to evoke similar thought patterns in the viewer to those created by Joyce's text in the reader. It is as if he has succeeded in tangling his own mental processes with those of Joyce, using his own craft of printmaking to produce a comparable wealth of imagery. His repeated use of the same plate, either in the primary form or as a derived second generation one, in different prints, serves to bind the whole suite together; the component image will be recognized from a previous print, but its use may change from the particular—for example representing Molly—to the universal, signifying womankind. His size variation (referred to by Morton Levitt in the commentary to "Blazes Boylan and Molly" (page 21)) delineates the viewpoint from which the print is derived. In a sense, the *Bloomsday Suite* relates to Joyce's *Ulysses* in much the same antiphonal fashion that *Ulysses* does to Homer's *Odyssey;* the source is recognizable; the treatment creates a work that stands on its own—but together they sing.

Field's prints open a new approach to the artist's book—taken together with Levitt's text they also provide the novice with a new route into a so-called "difficult" literary work. If the material in this book has the same effect on others that it has had on myself, it will give rise to many devoted Joyceans.

Robert Grigor-Taylor
Director, The Print Club
Philadelphia, May 1972

The illustrations in this book are reproduced from a portfolio of original embossed color engravings, hand pulled by Saul Field in his Willowdale studio and published by the Upstairs Gallery, Toronto, Ontario, Canada. The portfolio is a limited edition under the sponsorship of the following:
The James Joyce Foundation, Tulsa and Dublin
The University of Toronto Library, Rare Books
York University, Toronto
Sir George Williams University, Montreal
North York Public Library, Toronto
Toronto Public Library, Fine Arts Collection
Ronald Dzierbicki Collection, Detroit
St. Michael's College, Toronto
Roderique Lemay Collection, Ottawa
A portfolio has been acquired by each sponsoring collection. The edition is limited to 25. Each print is signed and numbered.
Saul Field gratefully acknowledges the interest and help of the sponsors and wishes also to thank the following institutions for the grants for his research on James Joyce:
The Canada Council, Ottawa
The Province of Ontario Council for the Arts, Toronto
The James Joyce Foundation, Tulsa and Dublin
The Samuel Paley Foundation, Philadelphia

I am indebted to several good friends—and good Joyceans as well—who were able and willing to offer help when I needed it on this endeavor: to J. Mitchell Morse, who first taught me my Joyce, and to Maurice Beebe and Sanford Pinsker, who read the manuscript with care. Their suggestions solved many problems for me, and they can hardly be blamed for those idiosyncrasies I was too obstinate to change.
From Jean and Saul Field and from Robert Grigor-Taylor, I learned more about art than I had ever known—and something about Joyce as well.
Above all, Annette Shandler Levitt, my best critic, listened patiently as I read and reread the separate pages and chapters of this book and resolved more problems than I can even remember. Much of what is best in this book, as in life, I owe to her.

M.P.L.